HANDY REFERENCE

To go to a Web page:
Enter the address in the Location bar, then press Return.

If you change your mind:
Abort the download by clicking Stop.

To turn off the images:
Deselect Auto Load Images (Options menu).

To load all the images on a page:
Click the Images button, or press Ctrl+I.

To load or save individual images:
Right-click on the icon or image, then select Load or
Save from the pop-up menu.

Keyboard shortcuts:

Ctrl+L	Open location
Ctrl+O	Open file
Ctrl+R	Reload
Ctrl+I	Load images
Alt+Cursor Left	Go back
Alt+Cursor Right	Go forwards
Ctrl+H	Open History window
Esc	Stop loading
Ctrl+D	Add bookmark
Ctrl+B	Open Bookmarks window
Ctrl+F	Find text
Ctrl+A	Select all
Ctrl+C	Copy selected text
Ctrl+V	Paste selected text
Ctrl+M	New Mail message

ABOUT THE SERIES

In easy steps series is developed for time-sensitive people who want results fast. It is designed for quick, easy and effortless learning.

By using the best authors in the field, and with our experience in writing computer training materials, this series is ideal for today's computer users. It explains the essentials simply, concisely and clearly - without the unnecessary verbal blurb. We strive to ensure that each book is technically superior, effective for easy learning and offers the best value.

Learn the essentials **in easy steps** - accept no substitutes!

Titles in the series include:

Title	Author	ISBN
Windows 95	Harshad Kotecha	1-874029-28-8
Microsoft Office	Stephen Copestake	1-874029-37-7
Internet UK	Andy Holyer	1-874029-31-8
CompuServe UK	John Clare	1-874029-33-4
CorelDRAW	Stephen Copestake	1-874029-32-6
PageMaker	Scott Basham	1-874029-35-0
Quicken UK	John Sumner	1-874029-30-X
Microsoft Works	Stephen Copestake	1-874029-41-5
Word	Scott Basham	1-874029-39-3
Excel	Pamela Roach	1-874029-40-7
Sage Sterling for Windows	Ralf Kirchmayr	1-874029-43-1
Sage Instant Accounting	Ralf Kirchmayr	1-874029-44-X
SmartSuite	Stephen Copestake	1-874029-42-3
HTML	Ralf Kirchmayr	1-874029-46-6
Netscape Navigator	Mary Lojkine	1-874029-47-4
PagePlus	Richard Hunt	1-874029-49-0
Publisher	Brian Austin	1-874029-56-3
Access	Stephen Copestake	1-874029-57-1

To order or for details on forthcoming titles ask your bookseller or contact Computer Step on 01926 817999.

NETSCAPE NAVIGATOR
in easy steps

Mary Lojkine

In easy steps is an imprint of Computer Step
5c Southfield Road, Southam
Warwickshire CV33 OJH England
☎01926 817999

First published 1996
Copyright © 1996 by Computer Step

Notice of Liability

Every effort has been made to ensure that this book contains accurate and current information. However, Computer Step and the author shall not be liable for any loss or damage suffered by readers as a result of any information contained herein.

Trademarks

Netscape, the Netscape logo and Mozilla are trademarks of Netscape Communications Corporation. Microsoft and Windows are registered trademarks of Microsoft Corporation. All other trademarks are acknowledged as belonging to their respective companies.

For all sales and volume discounts please contact Computer Step on Tel: 01926 817999.

For export orders and reprint/translation rights write to the address above or Fax: (+44) 1926 817005.

Printed and bound in the United Kingdom

ISBN 1-874029-47-4

Contents

1. Getting Started 7

Introduction to the Internet..........................8
Connecting to the Internet 10
Internet Service Providers 12
Connection Software 13
How to Get Navigator 14
Installing Navigator.................................16
Running Navigator 17
Entering Your Details 18
Buying a Licence....................................20

2. Basic Web Browsing 21

Areas of the Screen 22
Understanding URLs 23
Entering a URL 24
What If It Doesn't Work? 25
Using Links 26
Retracing Your Steps 27
Saving Web Pages 28
Copying Text....................................... 29
Copyright 30

3. Images 31

Turning Off the Images............................. 32
Loading, Viewing and Saving Images 33
Images as Links 34
Image Maps 35
Image Options 36

4. Exploring the Web 37

Directories 38
Search Engines 39
Best and Worst 40
News 41
Weather 43
Points of View 44
Entertainment 47
Sport 50
Home and Hearth 52
Travel Guides 54
Museums 55
Science 56
Computing 57
Service Providers 60

5. Bookmarks 61

Creating Bookmarks 62
Organising Your Bookmarks 63
Bookmark Folders 64
Special Bookmark Folders 65
Other Useful Tricks 66
The Bookmark File 68
Importing Bookmarks 69
Internet Shortcuts 70

6. Helper Applications 71

Helper Applications Explained 72
Setting up Helper Applications 73
Audio 74
Video 75
RTF and PDF Files 76
PostScript Files 77
Executable Files (Programs) 78
Compressed Files 79
Viruses 80

7. Intermediate Web Browsing 81

Finding Text 82
Reloading a Web Page 83
The History Window 84
New Windows 85
Directory Menu 86
Help Menu 87
Viewing HTML Codes 89
Document Information 90

8. Interactive Web Pages 91

Forms 92
Site Registration 93
Web Chat 94
Frames 95
Client-Pull Page Updates 97
Server-Push Animation 98
Java 99
JavaScript 100

9. Advanced Configuration 101

Appearance 102
Fonts 103
Colours 104
Cache 105
Connections and Proxics 106
Security 107

10. Plug-ins 109

Plug-ins Explained 110
Installing Plug-ins 111
RealAudio 112
Shockwave 113
Acrobat 114
Live3D 115
EarthTime 116

11. FTP and Gopher 117

FTP Explained 118
Connecting to FTP Sites 119
Downloading Files 120
Uploading Files 121
Useful FTP Sites 122
Gopher Explained 125
Connecting to Gopher Sites 126

12. Mail 127

E-mail Explained 128
Sending Mail 129
The Mail Window 131
Receiving Mail 133
On- and Off-line Mail 135
Attachments 136
The Address Book 138
Signature Files 140

13. Newsgroups 141

Newsgroups Explained 142
Getting Started 144
Subscribing to Newsgroups 145
Reading Messages 146
Posting Messages 147
Netiquette 148
FAQs 149
Smileys and Acronyms 150
Typical Newsgroups 151

Index 153

CHAPTER ONE

Getting Started

Before you can use Netscape Navigator, you'll need to know a little about the Internet. This chapter provides a brief introduction, then explains how to obtain, install and set up Netscape Navigator.

Covers

Introduction to the Internet 8

Connecting to the Internet 10

Internet Service Providers 12

Connection Software 13

How to Get Navigator 14

Installing Navigator 16

Running Navigator 17

Entering Your Details 18

Buying a Licence 20

Introduction to the Internet

The Internet is a 'network of networks' which connects millions of computers from all around the world. It's estimated that more than 40 million people have access to the Internet, and this number increases every day.

You can use the Internet to access general and specialist news services, research anything from aardvarks to zwitterions and find out more about your favourite sport, hobby, television programme or pop group. You can also send messages to people all around the world, participate in discussion groups and obtain software for your computer.

History of the Internet

The Internet has its roots in 1969, when the US Government decided to connect some of its computers so scientists and military agencies could communicate more easily. Because the Cold War dominated American politics at the time, the system was designed to withstand a nuclear attack. There was no central control centre; each machine operated independently and messages travelled from one computer to another by whatever route seemed most convenient.

In the 1970s several more computer networks were established by military and academic institutions. Eventually many of these networks were linked together, creating the network of networks we now know as 'the Internet'. Throughout the 1980s the Internet was dominated by scientists, academics, computer experts and students, but in the 1990s it has become accessible to a much wider range of people.

No one owns or controls the Internet and the infrastructure is somewhat shambolic. It can be creaky, cranky and intensely irritating, but for the most part everything works very well. You can connect to a computer in New York just as easily – and as cheaply – as to one in York, England. Although some parts of the world are better represented than others, the Internet is becoming a truly global phenomenon.

The World Wide Web

The recent surge of media interest in the Internet is mostly due to the World Wide Web. Developed in 1990 at CERN, the European Laboratory for Particle Physics, the Web consists of millions of magazine-style pages containing text and images, plus multimedia elements such as sound samples, animations and video clips.

'Browsing' the Web is a lot like using a multimedia CD-ROM, but the material you're looking at could come from anywhere on the Internet. The pages are connected together by hypertext links, enabling you to move from page to page by clicking on underlined text or highlighted images. You can also go directly to a particular page by typing in its address.

Web Browsers

In order to look at – or 'browse' – Web pages, you need a piece of software called a Web 'browser'. It enables you to find Web pages and display them on your screen.

The most popular Web browser is the one featured in this book, Netscape Navigator. Produced by Netscape Communications Corporation, it offers a wealth of features and is very easy to use. It's estimated that over 80 per cent of Web users use Navigator, and many Web pages are designed to take advantage of its special features.

Strictly speaking, Netscape is the company and Navigator is the program, but many people refer to the program as 'Netscape'. This book always calls it 'Navigator', to avoid confusion with Netscape's other products.

Connecting to the Internet

Before you can access the Web, you need to be connected to the Internet. There are three possibilities: your company or university may provide a direct connection; you can visit a cyber café; or you can use a modem (a device which enables computers to communicate with each other over a phone line) to connect your home computer to the Internet.

Company Connections

If you work for a university, or a large company that has an internal computer network, you may already be connected to the Internet. Buy your systems manager a drink and ask if it's possible for you to access the World Wide Web from your PC, Macintosh or workstation. He or she may be horrified by the prospect, but with a bit of luck you'll soon be exploring the Web.

The advantage of a company connection is that you don't have to pay for it. There are two disadvantages: you have to be at work to access the Internet, and you have no control over the speed of the connection, which can be anything from excellent to awful.

Cyber Cafés

The cyber café is the Internet equivalent of the public telephone, but generally warmer and more comfortable. You can drink coffee (or beer, in a cyber pub) and use the café's computers to explore the Internet. There are over 50 cyber cafés in the UK, with more opening every month.

Charges vary, but you can expect to pay around £2.50 for half an hour on the Internet. Some cafés also operate a membership system, enabling you to have your own e-mail address and send and receive messages.

If you aren't sure whether the Internet is for you, visiting a cyber café is a good way to get a feel for the services it offers. You don't have to worry about obtaining or installing software, and there's generally someone to help with any problems. You are, however, stuck with whatever software the café provides, and you can't set things up to suit your particular needs.

Dial-up Connections

The most versatile option is to use a modem to connect your home computer to the Internet. Regrettably, this is also the option which requires the most input – both financial and technical – from you.

You need five things to establish a dial-up connection:

1 A computer. Netscape Navigator is available for PCs, Apple Macintoshes and UNIX systems, but this book concentrates on the PC version. You can just about get by with a 386SX processor and 4Mb of RAM (6Mb for Windows 95), but you'll have a happier time if you're using a 486 or better with at least 8Mb of RAM. You also need to be running Windows 3.1, 3.11 or 95.

2 A modem. Modems come in two flavours – internal and external – and a range of speeds. It's a false economy to buy anything other than a 28,000bps (bits per second) modem; a slower modem may be cheaper, but you'll run up bigger phone bills.

You won't be able to receive phone calls while you're on-line, so you may want to invest in an answering service, such as BT's Call Minder.

3 A telephone line. If your phone company offers cheap deals on local calls, so much the better.

4 An Internet service provider (see page 12). A service provider has a computer system that is permanently connected to the Internet, and to a bank of modems. You use your modem to connect to one of the service provider's modems, via your telephone line, thereby making your computer (temporarily) part of the Internet.

5 Connection software. You'll need a TCP/IP utility to establish the connection (see page 13).

Internet Service Providers

Service providers enable you to connect to the Internet. Most also provide basic Internet software and help you set it up. There are two types of provider:

1   Regular service providers, such as Demon Internet or Direct Connection, simply enable you to connect to the Internet. They generally charge a flat monthly fee, no matter how much (or how little) time you spend on-line.

Unless your telephone line is supplied by a cable company that offers free local calls, you'll also be running up your phone bill while you're connected to the Internet.

2   On-line services, such as CompuServe, provide additional information services for their members. They generally charge according to the time you spend on-line, so they can be quite expensive if you use the Internet a lot.

Most Internet magazines publish up-to-date lists of Internet service providers. The things to consider when choosing a provider are:

1   Level of service. Make sure you'll be getting full Internet access, including e-mail, newsgroups and the Web.

2   Points of Presence (PoPs). Try to find a service provider which has an access point within your local call area, otherwise your phone bill will be astronomical.

3   Subscriber-to-modem ratio. If your service provider has lots of subscribers and hardly any modems, you'll find it difficult to get through. A ratio of 30:1 is passable, 15:1 is good.

4   Technical support. Call up and ask a few questions. If you can't understand the answers, try another provider.

Connection Software

Before you can run Netscape Navigator, or any other Internet application, you need to persuade your modem to connect your computer to the Internet. You do this with a small program called a winsock, which dials your modem and establishes a TCP/IP interface, enabling your other programs to send and receive data. TCP/IP stands for Transmission Control Protocol/Internet Protocol, but fortunately you don't ever need to know anything about it – your winsock takes care of all the technical bits.

You can't use a 32-bit version of Navigator unless you have a 32-bit winsock, such as Windows 95's built-in winsock.

Windows 95 has a built-in winsock. Unless you have the Microsoft Plus! add-on pack it's quite difficult to configure, but your service provider should be able to supply you with instructions.

If you have an earlier version of Windows, you'll need a separate winsock application. Your service provider will probably supply a shareware winsock, such as Trumpet Winsock. Once again, it should also be able to give you instructions for setting up the winsock – the details vary from service to service. Alternatively, you can also use the winsock from a commercial Internet software package.

Broadly speaking, 'log on' means to make a connection. As well as logging on to the Internet, you can log on to particular services. Conversely, 'log off' means to disconnect.

Once your winsock is configured correctly, you can use it to dial into your service provider's computer. Some winsocks send your user name and password automatically; others require you to enter these details each time you log on. You then leave the winsock running in the background while you run Netscape Navigator.

When you're finished browsing the Web, you close Navigator, then disconnect from the Internet by logging off and closing the winsock (if you're using Windows 95's built-in winsock, you simply click the Disconnect button).

How to Get Navigator

'Download' means to copy a file from a computer on the Internet to your computer. Uploading a file copies it from your computer to one on the Internet.

Most service providers will supply you with some start-up software, but you're unlikely to get a copy of Navigator, which is a commercial product. You can, however, download it from the Internet and 'evaluate' it for 90 days. Alternatively, you can purchase a copy outright.

Downloading Evaluation Versions

There are two options for downloading the software:

You can connect to Netscape's Web site, at:
`http://home.netscape.com/`
using whatever Web browser software your service provider supplied. If you skip ahead to Chapter Two, you'll find most of the 'Basic Browsing' instructions apply equally well to any other browser. Follow the instructions on the Netscape page to download Navigator.

Once your 90 days are up, you may be required to purchase a licence. See page 20 for details.

You can also use an older copy of Navigator to download a newer version, as shown here.

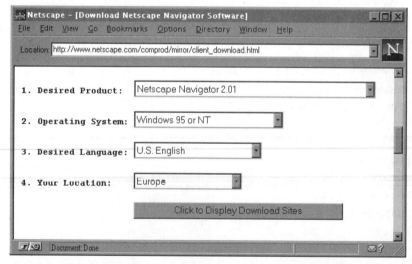

The latest version will take at least 15-20 minutes to download, even with a 28,800bps modem.

2 Your service provider may keep the latest version on a bulletin board or FTP site. This is often the best way to get a copy, because the Netscape Web pages are usually very busy. However, you will have to get to grips with a basic comms package, such as HyperTerminal, or an FTP client. Consult your documentation, which may provide a step-by-step guide, or call your service provider for advice.

Purchasing a Licensed Copy

If you'd rather just buy a copy, contact Unipalm PIPEX, Netscape's UK distributor. Generally you'll be offered a range of deals: you can buy Navigator with or without the manual (without is cheaper, obviously), and you may also be able to take out a subscription, entitling you to free upgrades for a year or so.

Unipalm PIPEX is also a service provider, so you'll find the number in any Internet magazine. You can also get more information about the latest deals from its Web site, at: http://www.unipalm.pipex.com/netscape/

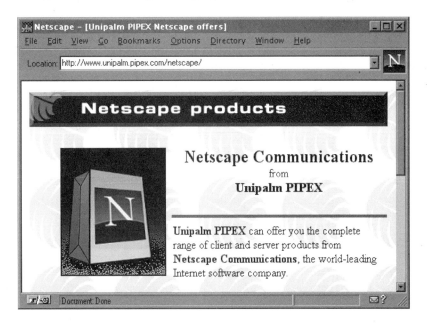

Installing Navigator

HANDY TIP

Navigator is upgraded every few months. This book was written for versions 2 and 3 – if you're still using version 1, upgrade!

Assuming you've chosen to download an evaluation copy, you'll end up with a file called something like n32e201.exe on your hard disk. The 32 at the beginning of the filename indicates that this is a 32-bit version for use with Windows 95; Windows 3.1 users should have a file that begins n16. The number at the end of the filename is the version number, which in this case is 2.01.

This file is a self-extracting archive – a compressed file which contains everything you need to install and run Navigator. To install the program itself, you must:

1 Use Explorer or File Manager to move this file to a folder (directory) other than the one you want the program to end up in. If you have a c:\temp folder, you can put it there.

2 Double-click on the filename. If you downloaded the Windows 95 version, the setup program will run automatically – just follow the on-screen instructions.

3 If you downloaded the Windows 3.1 version, double-clicking simply extracts the contents of the archive. Run the setup.exe program to install Navigator.

4 At the end of the setup routine you are asked if you want to connect to Netscape's setup site. Doing so enables you to register the software, purchase a licence and download plug-ins (see Chapter Ten). UK users will find it more convenient to purchase a licence from Unipalm PIPEX, so you may want to skip this step. You can also log on to this site at a later date by selecting Software from Navigator's Help menu.

Running Navigator

To run Navigator, simply double-click on its icon:

Windows 95 users will find the icon under Netscape in the Programs section of the Start menu, and possibly on the desktop as well; Windows 3.1 users will find it in a Netscape program group.

Navigator searches for your winsock program (see page 13) and runs it, enabling you to establish a connection to the Internet. Once you have logged on and are on-line, Navigator takes you to Netscape's Web site.

You must leave your winsock program running while you browse the Web. If you close it, your on-line session will come to an abrupt and untimely end.

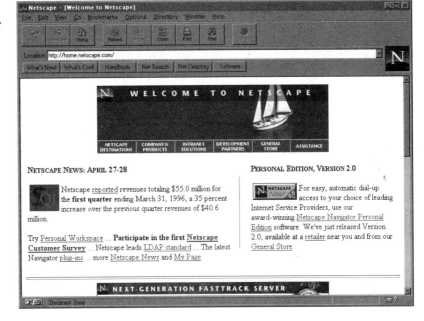

Strictly speaking, you don't have to close Navigator before you log off. Sometimes it's handy to leave it running – see page 28.

You are now browsing the Web!

To end your session, close Navigator by clicking in the Close box in the top right-hand corner of the window, or by pressing Ctrl+W. Switch to your winsock program, log off and close the winsock.

Entering Your Details

Navigator works perfectly well as a Web browser without any further configuration. However, if you want to use it to send e-mail (Chapter Twelve) or access Usenet newsgroups (Chapter Thirteen), you need to enter a few details.

1 Select Mail and News Preferences... from the Options menu and click on the Servers tab.

REMEMBER

You must enter the names exactly as they are shown on your information sheet. Unlike e-mail addresses, they don't contain an @ symbol.

2 Enter the names of your service provider's mail servers. These should be on the information sheets you received when you opened your account.

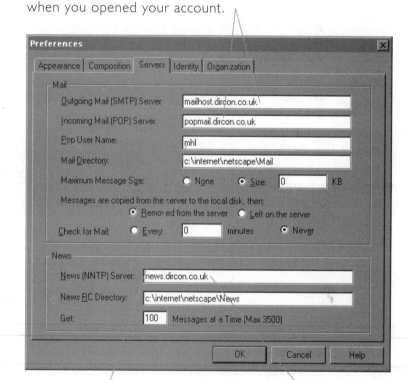

Preferences

Appearance | Composition | Servers | Identity | Organization

Mail

Outgoing Mail (SMTP) Server: `mailhost.dircon.co.uk`

Incoming Mail (POP) Server: `popmail.dircon.co.uk`

Pop User Name: `mhl`

Mail Directory: `c:\internet\netscape\Mail`

Maximum Message Size: ○ None ● Size: `0` KB

Messages are copied from the server to the local disk, then:
● Removed from the server ○ Left on the server

Check for Mail: ○ Every: `0` minutes ● Never

News

News (NNTP) Server: `news.dircon.co.uk`

News RC Directory: `c:\internet\netscape\News`

Get: `100` Messages at a Time (Max 3500)

[OK] [Cancel] [Help]

HANDY TIP

Your directory settings may be different from those shown here, because they are generated automatically. Unless your service provider is the same as mine – Direct Connection (see page 60) – the other details will also be slightly different.

3 Enter your POP mail user name. This is generally the first part of your e-mail address.

4 Enter the name of your service provider's news server.

...contd

5 Once all the information about your service provider is entered correctly, click on the Identity tab.

HANDY TIP

Some areas of the Internet are still very male-dominated, so women may want to use their initials or a pseudonym. You're unlikely to encounter any serious harassment, but you may find that male users insist on chatting you up instead of sticking to the 'official' topic of the newsgroup or discussion area.

6 Enter your name, or a pseudonym if you don't want other Internet users to know who you are.

7 Enter your e-mail address.

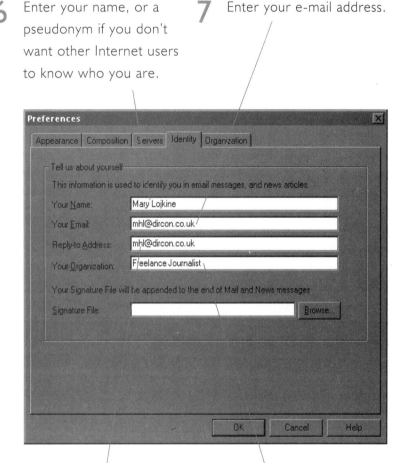

8 Unless you have more than one e-mail address, this entry is the same as the previous one.

9 If you belong to a company, or want people to know what you do, enter the details.

10 You don't need to bother about any of the other settings for now. Click OK to close the dialogue box.

Buying a Licence

Netscape Navigator is not freeware or shareware; it is a commercial product. Nevertheless, you may use it free of charge if:

> *"...your use of the Software is for the purpose of evaluating whether to purchase an ongoing license to the Software. The evaluation period for use by or on behalf of a commercial entity is limited to 90 days; evaluation use by others is not subject to this 90 day limit."*

(Netscape Navigator 2.01 licence)

The only exceptions are students, faculty and staff of educational institutions (including libraries) and employees of charitable non-profit organisations. Anyone falling into one of these categories can automatically use Navigator free of charge. However, you are not entitled to hard-copy documentation, support or technical assistance if you haven't paid for a licence.

HANDY TIP

While you're on the About Netscape... page, try clicking on the large Netscape logo in the top-left corner. You'll get a list of Navigator's authors.

These conditions and exceptions are subject to change, so you should check the latest version of the licence before assuming you can continue using the software. To do this, select About Netscape... from the Help menu. A Web page will appear; click the word 'license', which should be blue and underlined. The licence agreement for your version will appear in the main window.

The easiest way for UK users to purchase a licence is via Netscape's UK distributor, Unipalm PIPEX – see page 15 for details.

CHAPTER TWO

Basic Web Browsing

Netscape Navigator enables you to locate and view Web pages. This chapter gets you started.

Covers

Areas of the Screen 22

Understanding URLs 23

Entering a URL 24

What If It Doesn't Work? 25

Using Links 26

Retracing Your Steps 27

Saving Web Pages 28

Copying Text... 29

Copyright 30

Areas of the Screen

Like most Windows programs, Netscape Navigator has menu and tool bars across the top of the window, and a status line at the bottom. The most important areas of the screen are:

Link icon, for creating bookmarks (version 3 only) – see Chapter Five

Menu bar

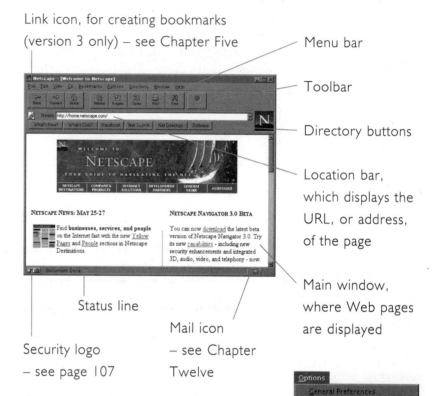

Toolbar

Directory buttons

Location bar, which displays the URL, or address, of the page

Main window, where Web pages are displayed

Status line

Mail icon – see Chapter Twelve

Security logo – see page 107

HANDY TIP

The Toolbar and Directory buttons are turned off in most of the screen grabs in this book, to show you more of the main window.

You can enlarge the main window by turning off the Toolbar, Location bar and Directory buttons.

1 Pull down the Options menu and click on the item you wish to turn off. Only 'ticked' items are displayed.

2 To reinstate an item, repeat Step 1 to turn it on again.

3 To make your changes permanent, select Save Options (version 2 only).

Understanding URLs

Every page on the Web has a unique address. These addresses are called Uniform Resource Locators, or URLs. You've probably already seen some URLs on television and in newspaper adverts.

A page is a single Web document. Some are quite long – use the scroll bar to move through them. A site is a collection of related pages, and the server is the computer on which all the documents are stored.

The URL for the page which lists all the software you can download from Netscape's Web site is:

http://home.netscape.com/comprod/mirror/index.html

The 'http:' indicates that this is a Web page.

This section tells your browser which directory the page is stored in.

This is the name of the server where the page is stored.

This is the name of the document which describes the page.

Web pages' URLs always begin with http: (it stands for HyperText Transfer Protocol). You may also come across URLs for other types of Internet site:

URL Begins	Type of Site	See Chapter
ftp:	FTP	Eleven
gopher:	Gopher	Eleven
mailto:	E-mail address	Twelve
news:	Usenet newsgroup	Thirteen

Abbreviated URLs

URLs for major sites are generally quite short. The URL for the Internet Movie Database (see page 47) is:

http://uk.imdb.com/

If the URL doesn't specify a particular document, Navigator automatically looks for an index file. As long as the person in charge of the Web site has provided one, the first two parts of the address are enough to locate the site.

Entering a URL

If you know the address of the Web page you wish to visit, you can simply enter it into your browser. There are two ways to do this:

 Sometimes it takes a while for Navigator to download and display a page. Check the Status line to find out what's happening, or look at the Netscape icon. If there are stars streaming across it, Navigator is still working. You can abort a download by clicking the Stop button or pressing the Esc key.

1 Type it into the Location bar (the word 'Location:' will change to 'Go to:' when you start typing), then press the Enter key. Netscape will find the page and display it.

2 If you have turned off the Location bar, you can enter URLs by clicking the Open button on the Toolbar, selecting Open Location… from the File menu or pressing Ctrl+L. All three actions bring up the Open Location dialogue box. Enter the URL and click the Open button.

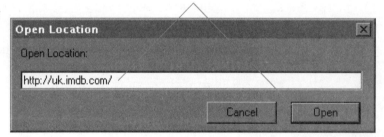

 Chapter Four contains some URLs for you to try. You'll also find lots of URLs in most Internet magazines.

You must get the URL absolutely right, otherwise Navigator won't be able to locate the page. In particular, make sure the capitalisation is correct – you can't substitute an 'a' for an 'A' – and don't let any spaces creep in. URLs never contain spaces.

What If It Doesn't Work?

The Internet is constantly evolving: sites come and go on a daily basis and servers are constantly being moved or upgraded. It's also subject to its fair share of bugs, glitches, crashes and bad connections. All this means that sometimes Navigator will give you an error message instead of displaying the page you were looking for.

The three most common error messages are:

HANDY TIP

You can sometimes find a page which has moved by entering part of the URL. Start by leaving out everything after the last slash (/). Navigator may then be able to locate an index page. If that doesn't work, keep chopping off sections until you get back to the name of the server (see page 23).

1 File Not Found. There are numerous variations on this message, but they all amount to one of two things: either you typed the URL incorrectly, or the page you were looking for has been moved or deleted.

> ## File Not found
>
> The requested URL /hello/hello.html was not found on this server.

2 No Response. This generally means the computer you were trying to reach is busy or off-line. Often these problems clear themselves quite quickly, so try again in a few minutes.

Netscape

⚠ Netscape is unable to locate the server: uk.imdb.com
The server does not have a DNS entry.

Check the server name in the Location (URL) and try again.

OK

REMEMBER

A domain name server converts the second part of the URL into a string of numbers, enabling Navigator to work out how to connect to a particular machine.

3 No DNS Entry. This sometimes means you've made a mistake in the second part of the URL. It can also indicate a problem with your service provider's domain name server, or with your connection. Try again, then try hanging up and reconnecting.

Netscape

⚠ There was no response. The server could be down or is not responding.

If you are unable to connect again later, contact the server's administrator.

OK

Using Links

If you could only get to Web pages by typing in their URLs, browsing the Web would be tedious and time-consuming. Fortunately there's a much easier way to get about: links.

Almost every Web page is linked to anything from one to a hundred or more other pages. Links are usually indicated by coloured, underlined text, and you move to the linked page by clicking on this text. For example:

I Here's a page from the BBC's Web site (see page 48). If you click on the blue (take my word for it) underlined text that says 'Films'...

2 ...you are taken to this page, which lists the week's movies.

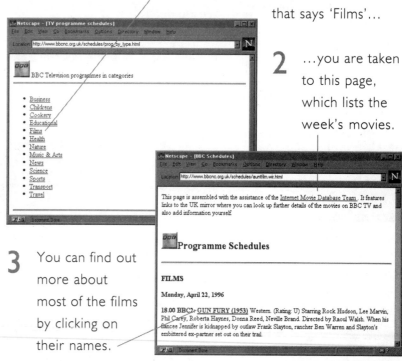

3 You can find out more about most of the films by clicking on their names.

HANDY TIP

You can change the colour of the links and/or remove the underlining – see pages 102 and 104.

Links are usually blue, or purple if you've clicked on them recently, but they can be other colours. However, you can always tell when the mouse pointer is over a link, because it changes into a pointing hand. While you're pointing, check the Status line to see the address of the page at the other end of the link.

Pictures can also be used as links – see pages 34–5.

Retracing Your Steps

By now you'll have realised that browsing the Web is like exploring the back streets of an old market town – there are lots of directions to head in and it's easy to get lost. Fortunately, it's equally easy to retrace your steps.

1 To go back to a page you visited recently, click on the Back button, select Back from the Go menu or press Alt+Cursor Left.

2 Once you've gone back a few pages, you may want to go forward again. Click on the Forward button, select Forward from the Go menu, or press Alt+Cursor Right.

3 You can speed up the process using the Go menu, which lists the 10–15 pages you've visited most recently. Just select the name of the page you want to return to.

REMEMBER **Your Home page is the page Navigator searches for each time you run it. If you do a lot of exploring, you may want to make one of the search engines (see page 39) your Home page. Confusingly, the term 'Home page' is also used to describe a personal Web page, or the main page of a company site.**

4 If you get completely lost, you can return to your Home page by clicking on the Home button or selecting Home from the Go menu. The default Home page is Netscape's main Web page, but you can change this to anything you like. Select General Preferences... from the Options menu, click on the Appearance tab and enter the URL of your favourite page in the Startup section.

Saving Web Pages

HANDY TIP

If you're only going to read a page once, there's no need to save it – just log off without closing Navigator. The page will still be loaded and you can scroll through it as usual.

HANDY TIP

You can also print a page, complete with its images, by selecting Print from the File menu.

Sometimes you'll want to read a lengthy Web page at your leisure, without worrying about your phone bill, or to keep the information handy for reference. The easiest solution is to save it onto your hard disk. You can then reload it whenever you want, without connecting to the Internet.

1 To save a Web page, pull down the File menu and select Save As..., or press Ctrl+S. This brings up the standard Save As dialogue box. Note that this only saves the text; if you want the pictures as well, you have to save them separately – see page 33.

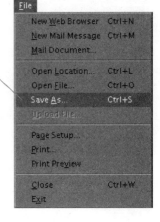

2 To reload a saved page, select Open File... from the same menu, or press Ctrl+O.

Off-line Browsing

Windows 95 users can run Navigator without connecting to the Internet – simply click the Cancel button when it tries to run your winsock, then click the Stop button or press Esc. Alternatively, tell Navigator to start with a blank page. It then won't bother running your winsock.

Select General Preferences... from the Options menu, click on the Appearance tab and select Start With: Blank Page.

This doesn't work under Windows 3.1 – even if you only want to load a saved page, you still have to log on to run Navigator. You can log off again immediately, though.

Copying Text

You can move text from Navigator to your word processor using the Copy and Paste commands. This is handy if you want to quote from a Web page in an article or project. It's also an easy way to make notes.

1 Drag the mouse over the text you want to copy, such as this passage from the NBA Web site (see page 51). Select Copy from the Edit menu, or press Ctrl+C.

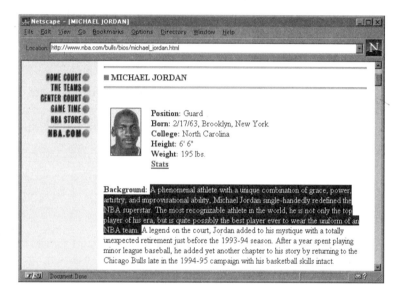

2 Switch to your word processor and select Paste from the Edit menu, or press Ctrl+V.

Don't forget to credit the site – text on Web pages is subject to copyright. See overleaf for details.

> A phenomenal athlete with a unique combination of grace, power,¶
>   artistry, and improvisational ability, Michael Jordan single-handedly redefined the¶
>   NBA superstar. The most recognizable athlete in the world, he is not only the top¶
>   player of his era, but is quite possibly the best player ever to wear the uniform of an¶
>   NBA team.¶

The pasted text has some extra carriage returns and spaces, but removing these is less work than retyping everything.

Copyright

Text and images on the Web are protected by copyright, just like the text and images in a book. The fact that it's technically possible to save them onto your hard disk, load them into other applications and reuse them doesn't mean you can legitimately do so.

In practice, you're unlikely to have the police banging on your door at midnight if you keep copies of your favourite articles and images on your hard disk, even though strictly speaking you may be in breach of copyright. If, however, you download images willy-nilly and make commercial use of them, you may end up in serious trouble. You certainly shouldn't upload anything that isn't your own work.

Copyright law is very complex, and it's beyond the scope of this book to provide in-depth advice. If you have any doubts about the legality of your on- and off-line activities, consult an expert.

CHAPTER THREE

Images

One of the things that makes the Web different from any other Internet service is its support for pictures. This chapter explains how to make the most of them.

Covers

Turning Off the Images 32

Loading, Viewing and Saving Images 33

Images as Links 34

Image Maps 35

Image Options 36

Turning Off the Images

HANDY TIP

The Web is like the M25 – the busier it gets, the slower everything moves. It's more responsive in the mornings, when all the North Americans are still in bed.

Images make Web pages colourful and user-friendly, but they also slow things down. Whereas text files are compact and download in a few seconds, image files are typically five to ten times larger and take proportionately longer to download. If you're prepared to make do with the words, you can speed everything up by turning off the images.

Pull down the Options menu and deselect Auto Load Images...

2 ...to turn the graphical Welcome page of Grooves (see page 49)...

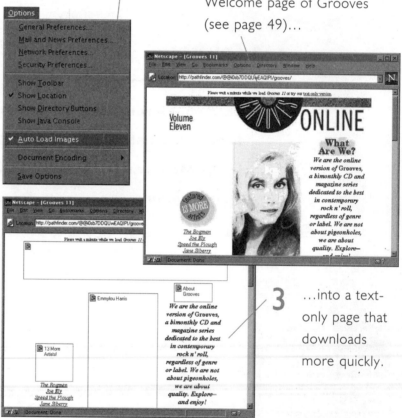

HANDY TIP

Many sites – including Grooves – provide text-only alternatives to graphic-intensive pages. Look out for a 'text-only version' link on the opening page.

3 ...into a text-only page that downloads more quickly.

The little icons [icon] show you where the pictures would normally be. Sometimes you'll also see some text to the right of the icon, telling you what you'd see if you turned the pictures on again.

About
Grooves

Loading, Viewing and Saving Images

Turning off the images may seem like a big compromise, but it does enable you to move around the Web a lot more quickly. And once you've found an interesting page, you can easily turn them on again – all at once, or selectively.

1   To download and display all the images on a page, click the Images button, select Load Images from the View menu or press Ctrl+I.

2   To download and display a single image, click on its icon with the right mouse button. A pop-up menu appears; select Load Image. (View Image loads the picture into the top-left corner of a blank Web page rather than displaying it in its proper place.)

3   Sometimes all you'll get is a 'broken' icon. This means Navigator can't find the image file. There's nothing you can do except wait for the author to fix the page.

REMEMBER

Images on Web pages are subject to copyright, just like images in books – see page 30 for more details.

4   You can also save images onto your hard disk. Right-click on the image, then select Save Image as… from the pop-up menu. This brings up the standard Windows Save As dialogue box.

Images as Links

An image can also be a link to another page. The three most common types of image links are:

1. Buttons. Many Web pages, including Microsoft's (see page 57) use toolbar-style buttons to make it easy for you to find your way around the site.

What's New Search Index FAQ Help Feedback

2. Thumbnails. Clicking on a small picture often takes you to a larger version of the same image. This is courtesy on the part of the page's designer – you can examine the small version before spending a minute or more downloading the full-size image.

3. Logos. There's no hard and fast rule on this one, but if a company's logo appears on every page of its Web site, clicking on it will usually take you back to the main page.

There are two ways to tell whether an image is a link:

1. By its border. Just as text links are usually blue and underlined (see page 26), many linked images have a blue border.

2. By the change in the pointer. Web page designers sometimes turn off the blue border to improve the appearance of the page. However, if you move the mouse pointer over a linked image, it changes into a pointing hand, indicating that clicking will take you to another page.

Image Maps

Some images contain more than one link. For example, the opening image on the MGM/UA site (see page 47) looks like a regular picture, but clicking on one of the film posters takes you to the appropriate section of the site.

If you aren't sure whether you're looking at an image map, check the Status line. If you see two numbers that change as you move the mouse over the image, it's a map.

This type of image is called an image map, because different sections of the picture are 'mapped' to different Web page addresses.

Occasionally you'll come across a page that appears to contain nothing but images; chances are one of them is an image map. If you're browsing with the images off, you'll need to click the Images button and load the image map to find out where you can go.

Image Options

As well as simply turning the images on and off, you can fine-tune their display.

1   Pull down the Options menu, select General Preferences... and click on the Images tab.

2   If you have a HighColour (16-bit) or TrueColour (24-bit) display, leave Choosing Colors: set to Automatic. If you run Windows in 256-colour mode, you can select Dither to make Navigator display colours more accurately, or Substitute Colors to speed things up.

You'll notice that some images appear from the top down, line by line, while others start off 'blocky' and gradually become more detailed. This depends on the image format rather than anything you can set in Navigator.

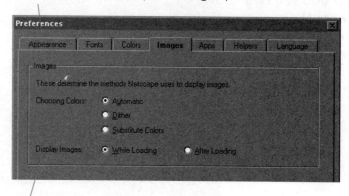

3   You'll almost certainly want Display Images: set to While Loading, so you can see how things are going and abort the transfer if you're in the wrong place or have selected the wrong image. Selecting After Loading sometimes produces faster results, but the lack of feedback means you lose more than you gain.

CHAPTER FOUR

Exploring the Web

The Internet has so much to offer that it's hard to know where to start. The best way to learn about the Web is by exploring it, so here's a selection of useful, interesting and entertaining sites that provide a good introduction.

Covers

Directories...38

Search Engines 39

Best and Worst..40

News..41

Weather 43

Points of View...44

Entertainment 47

Sport..50

Home and Hearth 52

Travel Guides 54

Museums 55

Science 56

Computing 57

Service Providers...60

Directories

Yahoo!
http://www.yahoo.com/

Most of the sites featured in this chapter are large, well-established and unlikely to move or vanish. If you do find that one of the addresses is no longer valid, you may still be able to find the site using a directory or search engine.

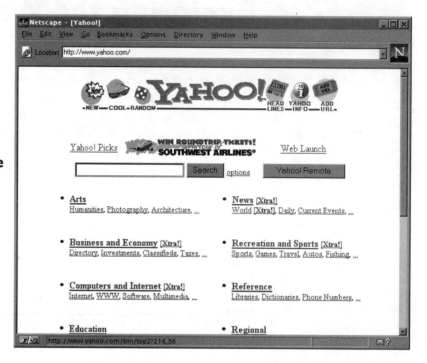

Yahoo! is a hierarchical directory of Web pages and (some) other Internet resources. Each of the 14 categories is progressively subdivided into more tightly defined subcategories, enabling you to work your way down to a list of Web sites that concentrate on your area of interest. It's extensively cross-referenced and very easy to use.

You could also try:

YELL, a UK Web directory brought to you by Yellow Pages. It's nowhere near as comprehensive as Yahoo!, but it's handy if you're looking for UK sites. Find it at: http://www.yell.co.uk/

Search Engines

Alta Vista
http://www.altavista.digital.com/

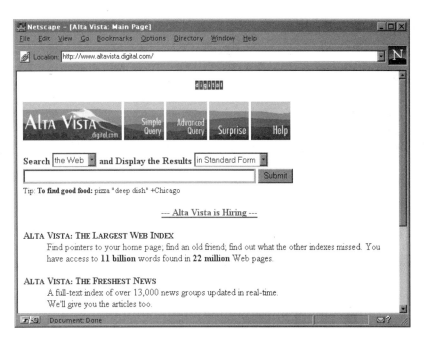

If you're new to the Web, or exploring a broad subject area, use one of the directories; if you want to find a specific piece of information quickly, use a search engine.

Alta Vista enables you to search for Web sites and Usenet newsgroups containing a particular word or phrase. It takes some practice to get the best out of it – it's easy to make your search too broad, producing thousands of hits – but it does enable you to find information very quickly.

You could also try:
Lycos, which provides a very similar service, although it doesn't cover newsgroups. Lycos also offers a Yahoo!-style hierarchical directory, a2z. Find it at:
http://www.lycos.com/

Best and Worst

Point
http://www.pointcom.com/gifs/home/

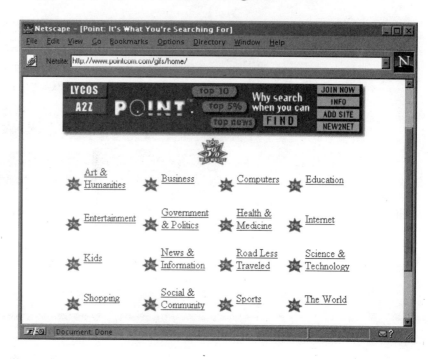

There are many amusing, unusual and downright odd sites on the Web. These services will help you track them down.

A sister site to Lycos (see page 39), Point reviews and rates the top five per cent of Web sites. Its listings are a good place to start if you find the all-embracingness of Yahoo! (see page 38) daunting.

You could also try:

Cool Site of the Day, for a daily pointer to a site worth your attention, at:
`http://cool.infi.net/`

Mirsky's Worst of the Web, for a regular round-up of tat, trash and bad ideas, complete with acidic commentary, at:
`http://mirsky.com/wow/Worst.html`

Useless World Wide Web Pages, for an overview of all things pointless, at:
`http://www.chaco.com/useless/`

News

PA NewsCentre
http://www.pa.press.net/

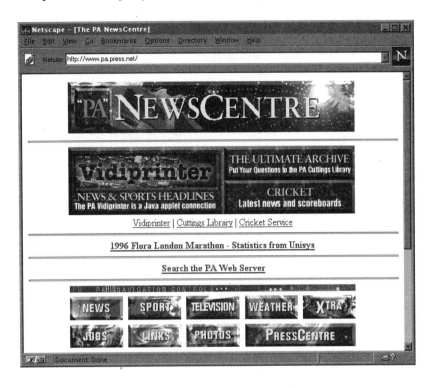

Many large sites require you to register before you can access any of the information - see page 93.

The PA NewsCentre site draws on the information gathered by the Press Association's news agencies. You get news headlines on the hour, a round-up of the day's papers, sports news, television and radio schedules and weather forecasts. There's generally more breadth than depth, but it's good for an up-to-the-minute overview.

You could also try:
The Electronic Telegraph, generally regarded as the best on-line version of a British broadsheet. It provides everything you'd expect from a 'proper' paper, including cartoons and a crossword. You can also search the archives, which go back to November 1994. Find it at:
`http://www.telegraph.co.uk/`

CNN Interactive
http://www.cnn.com/

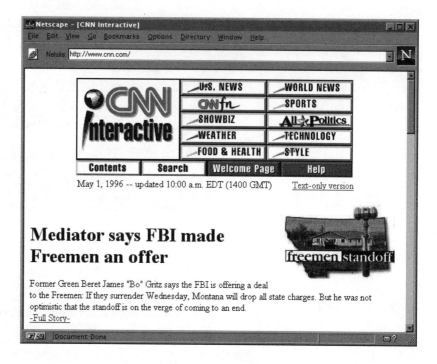

One of the great things about the Internet is the tremendous choice of viewpoints. Rather than sticking to British news sites, for example, why not pop over to the States for an American perspective on US and world news? CNN's site provides a wide range of clearly presented, cross-referenced stories, plus a searchable archive.

You could also try:
USA Today, the on-line version of the USA's biggest-selling general interest paper. Find it at:
http://www.usatoday.com/

TimesFax, an eight-page mini-edition of the *New York Times,* distributed as an Adobe PDF file (see page 76). Browse through it on your screen or print it out to read in comfort. Find it at:
http://nytimesfax.com/

Weather

The Met Office
http://www.meto.govt.uk/

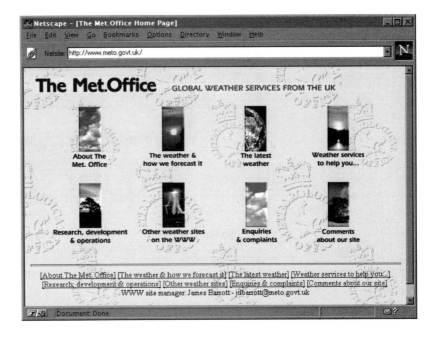

As the introduction reminds you, "in the UK, everyone talks about the weather." This site certainly provides plenty for you to talk about, but it's a bit thin on the predictive front – the Met Office's obligation to develop commercial services means there aren't any regional forecasts. You do get the UK 24-hour forecast, though, plus the inshore waters and shipping forecasts.

You could also try:
The PA NewsCentre and The Electronic Telegraph (see page 41) both carry more extensive forecasts – which, ironically, are supplied by the Met Office.

Points of View

Politics USA
http://PoliticsUSA.com/

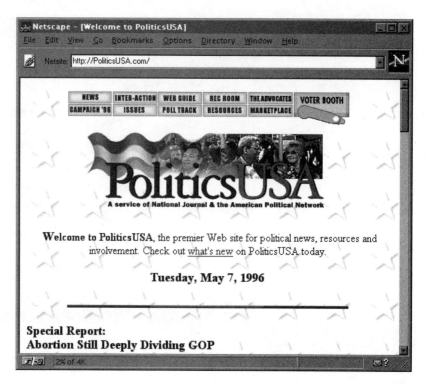

As you might expect, Politics USA reports on and analyses the American political situation. It aims to provide a balanced view of the issues and enables voters to pose questions and register their opinions. UK readers can follow the links to other on-line resources for more information about the American political system.

You could also try:

The Conservative Party, at:
http://www.conservative-party.org.uk/

The Labour Party, at:
http://www.poptel.org.uk/labour-party/

The Liberal Democrats, at:
http://www.libdems.org.uk/

HotWired
http://www.hotwired.com/

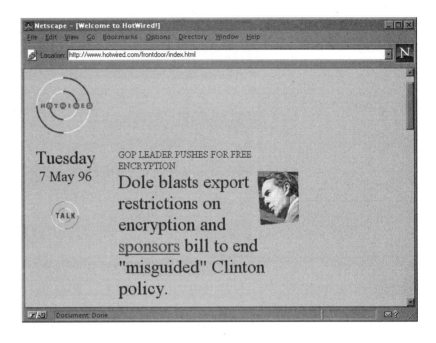

HANDY TIP

On-line magazines are often referred to as 'e-zines'. Some e-zines have paper equivalents, but many exist only on the Web.

The US version of *Wired* magazine reflects and shapes Internet culture; HotWired is its on-line offshoot. It covers politics, popular culture, technology and the Internet, and takes itself very seriously. HotWired can be somewhat impenetrable, but it's tremendously authoritative.

You could also try:
For a UK perspective on the Internet, try the on-line versions of *.net* and *Internet.* Find them, respectively, at:
```
http://www.futurenet.co.uk/netmag/net.html
http://www.emap.com/internet/
```

Women's Wire
http://www.women.com/

Women's Wire is an intelligent e-zine aimed primarily at career women. Sections include news, entertainment, careers, style and health and fitness, and you can e-mail questions to the site's panel of experts. The presentation is very professional and it's a good read.

You could also try:

A Man's Life, a men's magazine which provides "complete instructions for health and wealth". It's less career-oriented than Women's Wire and covers everything from women and clothes to money and sport. Find it at:
`http://www.manslife.com/`

Entertainment

The Internet Movie Database
http://uk.imdb.com/

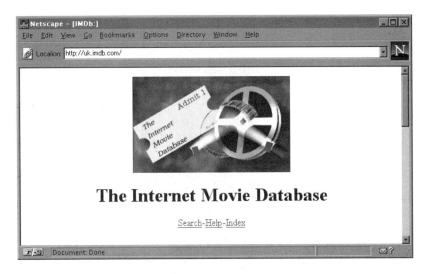

Containing pretty much everything you're likely to want to know about over 70,000 movies, The Internet Movie Database is the first place to go if you're looking for film-related information. As well as providing cast lists, synopses and reviews, it has links to everything from official studio sites to fan pages for directors and actors.

You could also try:

Most of the major studios and distributors have extensive Web sites. You'll find plenty to see and do at:

MCA/Universal Pictures, at: `http://www.mca.com/`
MGM/UA, at: `http://www.mgmua.com/motionpictures/`
Miramax, at: `http://www.miramax.com/`
Paramount, at: `http://www.paramount.com/`
Walt Disney, at: `http://www.disney.com/`

YELL (see page 38) has a film-finding service with programme details for 450 UK cinemas.

The BBC
http://www.bbcnc.org.uk/

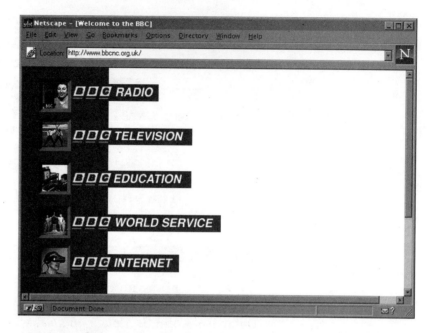

Aunty Beeb's site has back-up material for a selection of television and radio programmes, including *Blue Peter, Watch Out, Woman's Hour* and *The Net*. You can also find out what's on the box – or the air – this week.

You could also try:

Channel 4 Programme Support Online, for some of the supplementary information from its after-show booklets, plus links to programme-related sites. Find it at:
`http://www.c4support.bss.org/`

Sky Internet, an extensive Web site with schedules, news, sport and programme-related material. Find it at:
`http://www.sky.co.uk/`

Many popular programmes have their own Web sites. Use Yahoo! or YELL (see page 38) to find your favourites.

Grooves
http://pathfinder.com/grooves/

It's hard to find a music site with something for everyone, but Grooves comes pretty close. It concentrates on contemporary rock, regardless of genre, and combines extensive well-written commentary with sound samples and attractive graphics.

You could also try:

Classic CD, for extracts from the magazine of the same name, a beginner's guide to classical music and a list of music-related Web sites. Find it at:
`http://www.futurenet.co.uk/music/classiccd.html`

Jazz Online, an interactive publication specialising in jazz, blues, new age and world music. Find it at:
`http://www.jazzonln.com/`

Sport

Soccernet
http://www.soccernet.com/

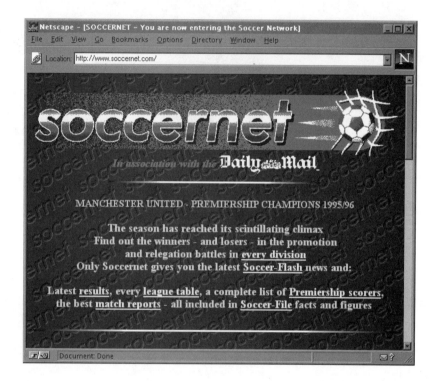

Produced in association with the *Daily Mail*, Soccernet provides news, results, league tables, match reports, gossip and lots of football trivia. It concentrates on the Premier League and has extensive information pages for the top 16 teams, but gives results for all the English and Scottish divisions.

You could also try:
CricInfo, the self-styled "home of cricket on the Internet". Based, surprisingly, in the United States, it covers all international, first-class and one-day domestic cricket worldwide and provides news, scorecards, match reports, statistics, player profiles and other cricket-related information. Find it at:
http://www.cricket.org/

National Basketball Association
http://www.nba.com/

Having access to the Internet makes it easy to follow sports that aren't popular in the UK, such as baseball, basketball, ice hockey and Australian Rules football. The NBA site features sound samples, video clips and interviews as well as news, previews, results and profiles, and while it isn't quite as good as being there, it's a truly excellent site.

You could also try:

Fastball, for Major League baseball, at:
`http://www.fastball.com/`

NHL Open Net, home of the National Hockey League, at:
`http://www.nhl.com/`

Grandstand, Web site of the Australian Football League, at:
`http://www.cadability.com.au/AFL/`

Home and Hearth

Electronic Gourmet Guide
http://www.2way.com/food/egg/

eGG is a well-established culinary e-zine featuring articles, columns, recipes, tips and food trivia. It's American, so you may need to 'translate' some of the ingredients, but the leisurely writing style makes it an enjoyable read.

You could also try:
Wine & Dine, a British e-zine covering food, wine and – somewhat less obviously – travel. Find it at:
http://www.winedine.co.uk/

The Rec.Food.Recipes Archive, which contains hundreds of recipes from the newsgroup of the same name. Find it at:
http://www.cs.cmu.edu/~mjw/recipes/

The Virtual Garden
http://pathfinder.com/vg/

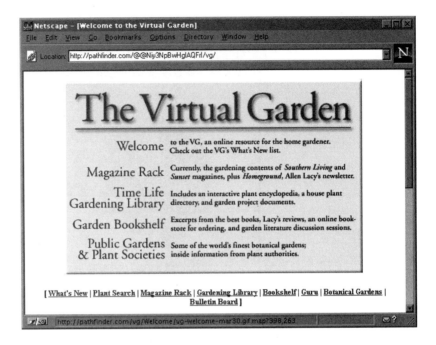

One of the many subsections of Time Warner's Pathfinder site, The Virtual Garden features extracts from various magazines, book reviews and information from the New York Botanical Garden and the American Orchid Society. Its best feature, though, is the gardening library, which comprises a searchable database of plants, a house plant database and a collection of project sheets.

Travel Guides

Japan Travel Updates
http://www.jnto.go.jp/

All distances are pretty much equal on the Web, so a site in
Japan is as easy to reach as a site just down the road. If you're
planning a real trip, Japan Travel Updates is probably the
best place to start, because it covers everything from things
to bring and places to stay to special events and festivals.

You could also try: ˙

New Zealand on the Web, which takes you about as far
from the UK as you can feasibly get and offers an illustrated
tour of the 'land of the long white cloud'. Find it at:
`http://nz.com/NZ/`

You can find tourist sites for almost every country in the
world in the Regional section of Yahoo! (see page 38). If
you're just looking for facts and figures, try the 1995 CIA
World Fact Book, at:
`http://www.odci.gov/cia/publications/95fact/`

Museums

Natural History Museum
http://www.nhm.ac.uk/

As well as providing information about opening times and current exhibitions, The Natural History Museum's site enables you to go behind the scenes and find out about some of the museum's on-going research projects. The interactive science casebooks are particularly impressive and should appeal to most children.

You could also try:
The Science Museum, at:
http://www.nmsi.ac.uk/

Portico, the British Library's on-line information service, at:
http://portico.bl.uk/

Science

Planet Science
http://www.newscientist.com/

Planet Science is an offshoot of *New Scientist* magazine. You don't need to be a boffin to enjoy it, because it's written in layman's language and has plenty of material on the science of everyday life – including the answers to vexing questions like how long to leave a fizzy drink after you've shaken the can. You'll also find news, features, reviews and comment from the magazine.

You could also try:
The NASA Home Page, gateway to a vast collection of information about space and space exploration. Highlights include the latest images from the Hubble telescope, day-by-day coverage of shuttle missions and a huge, searchable archive of space pictures. Find it at:
`http://www.gsfc.nasa.gov/`

Computing

Microsoft
http://www.microsoft.com/

Microsoft's Web site is much like Microsoft itself – huge. There's lots of information on the company's products, and you can download demos and add-ons. You can also access the Knowledge Base for answers to technical questions and 'how-to' articles that help you get more from your software.

You could also try:

Most software and hardware companies have Web sites. Use a search engine to find a particular company, or try:

Adobe, at: `http://www.adobe.com/`
Symantec, at: `http://www.symantec.com/`
Hewlett Packard, at : `http://www.hp.com/`
Hayes, at: `http://www.hayes.com/`
US Robotics, at: `http://www.usr.com/`

Netscape
http://home.netscape.com/

You can't really miss Netscape's page, because a default installation of Navigator takes you here automatically. Even if you've changed your Home page (see page 27), it's worth checking back regularly, if only to download the latest upgrade. Netscape's site also provides information about the company's products and showcases forthcoming developments in Internet technology.

You could also try:

Quarterdeck, one of Netscape's main rivals in the Internet software market. Check out its products at:
`http://www.qdeck.com/`

Computer Manuals On-line Bookstore
http://www.compman.co.uk/

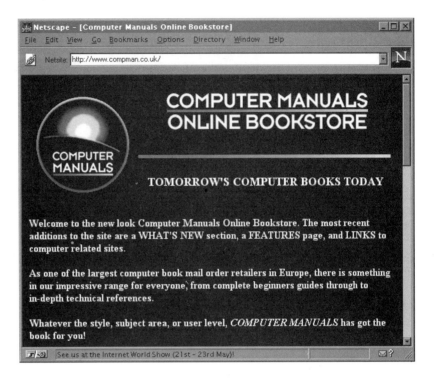

With over 5,000 books, CD-ROMs and videos in its catalogue, Computer Manuals is one of Europe's largest mail order retailers of computer books. Once you've found a suitable title, you can order it on-line or by telephone.

You could also try:
Most publishers of computer magazines have Web sites, featuring excerpts and extra (generally Internet-related) material. Three of the biggest are:

Emap, at: `http://www.emap.co.uk/`
Future Publishing, at: `http://www.futurenet.co.uk/`
Ziff Davis, at: `http://www.zdnet.com/`

Use YELL (see page 38) to track down other publishers and individual magazines.

Service Providers

Direct Connection
http://www.dircon.co.uk/

Finally, don't forget to check out your service provider's Web site, which may provide technical support as well as details of its services. For example, my service provider, Direct Connection, maintains lists of Internet resources and useful starting points. You can also access the personal Home pages of many of its members.

You could also try:

Check the information you were sent when you opened your account for the address of your service provider's site. Alternatively, inetuk maintains a list of providers in the UK and Ireland, with links to their Web sites. Find it at: `http://www.limitless.co.uk/inetuk/ providers.html`

CHAPTER FIVE

Bookmarks

Bookmarks enable you to keep track of your favourite Web sites and go back to them easily.

Covers

Creating Bookmarks 62

Organising Your Bookmarks 63

Bookmark Folders 64

Special Bookmark Folders 65

Other Useful Tricks 66

The Bookmark File 68

Importing Bookmarks 69

Internet Shortcuts 70

Creating Bookmarks

As you explore the Web, you'll often come across sites that you may want to visit again in the future. Rather than writing down the URL, you can have Netscape make a note of it. These notes are called 'bookmarks', because they enable you to return to a page you were looking at earlier, but really they are more like entries in an address book. Rather than being attached to the 'marked' Web page, they are stored in a file on your hard disk.

HANDY TIP

If there's any chance you might want to return to a site, bookmark it. Deleting unwanted bookmarks is much easier than retracing your steps.

1 To bookmark a Web page, pull down the Bookmark menu and select Add Bookmark, or press Ctrl+D.

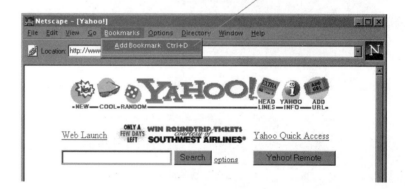

2 To return to the bookmarked site, go back to the Bookmark menu and select it from the list.

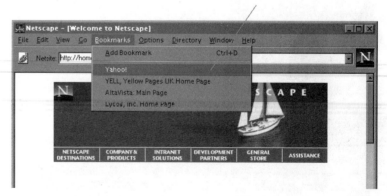

Navigator will jump straight to the selected page, just as if you had clicked on a link.

Organising Your Bookmarks

Your bookmark list will soon become unmanageably large and hopelessly disorganised. Here's how to sort it out.

 Each purple bookmark icon in the Bookmarks window corresponds to an entry on the Bookmarks menu.

1 Select Bookmarks from the Window menu, or press Ctrl+B, to open the Bookmarks window.

2 To remove a bookmark, click on it and select Delete from the Edit menu, or press the Delete key.

3 To move a bookmark, select it, then hold down the mouse button and drag it up or down the list. It will reappear immediately below the bookmark which is highlighted when you let go of the mouse button.

 The default name for a bookmark is the title of the page, which appears in square brackets in the top border of the Navigator window.

4 To rename a bookmark, click on it, then select Properties from the Item menu. Alternatively, right-click on the bookmark you want to change and select Properties from the pop-up menu. Enter the new name in the Name: box.

5 You can also add notes in the Description box.

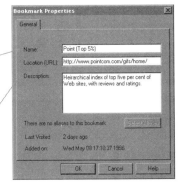

Bookmark Folders

Putting your bookmarks into folders makes it easier to find what you're looking for. You can create folders for all the family, or organise your bookmarks by subject.

HANDY TIP

You can also insert separators, horizontal lines which are used to divide groups of bookmarks. Click on the bookmark that the line should go beneath, then select Insert Separator from the Item menu.

1 To create a new folder, open the Bookmarks windows and click on the folder at the very top of the list. Select Insert Folder from the Item menu to bring up the Properties box. Name your folder, then click OK.

Top folder

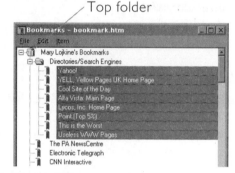

2 Use the mouse to drag bookmarks into the folder. You can move several at once by holding down the Shift key when you select them.

3 Click the ⊞ and ⊟ boxes to open and close your folders. You can also use the mouse to drag one folder into another, or to sort them. Drag them onto the folder at the very top, one at a time, until they are in the right order.

4 When you pull down the Bookmark menu and select a folder, a second menu appears to one side, enabling you to select one of the bookmarks.

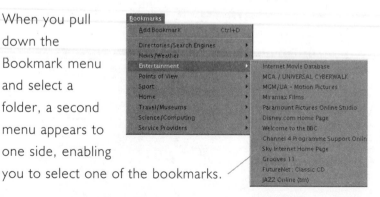

Special Bookmark Folders

New Bookmarks Folder

When you create a new bookmark, it is added to whichever folder has been specified as the New Bookmarks folder. Initially this is the folder at the top, but you can tell Navigator to put them somewhere else instead.

 The easiest way to get everything in the right place is to create a folder called 'New Bookmarks' and make it the New Bookmarks folder. You can drag all the new bookmarks to their proper places when you've finished browsing.

1 Open the Bookmarks window and select the folder you want to use for new bookmarks.

2 Select Set to New Bookmarks Folder from the Item menu. Alternatively, right-click on the folder and select Use for New Bookmarks from the pop-up menu (version 3 only).

3 A bookmark icon is added to the folder icon. New bookmarks will now be placed in this folder.

Bookmarks Menu Folder

Rather than listing all your bookmarks on the Bookmark menu, you can display just the contents of one folder – perhaps the folder containing the sites you visit most often.

1 Click on the folder you want to use and select Set to Bookmarks Menu Folder from the Item menu, or right-click and select Use for Bookmarks Menu (version 3 only).

2 A menu icon is added to the folder icon. The Bookmark menu now only lists the bookmarks from this folder.

Other Useful Tricks

Side-by-Side Browsing

If you run Windows in a high-resolution screen mode (say, 1024 x 768), try placing the Bookmarks window alongside the main Navigator window. You can then jump to a bookmarked page by double-clicking on it in the Bookmarks window. If you have Navigator 3, you can create bookmarks by dragging the link icon to the Bookmarks window.

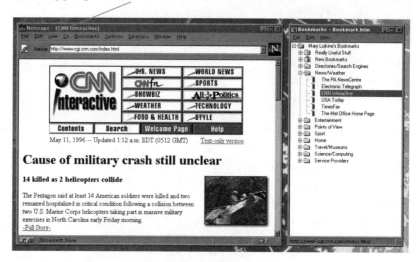

What's New?

You can find out whether any of your bookmarked pages have changed by selecting What's New? from the File menu of the Bookmarks window. Generally it's best to select a group of bookmarks first, because checking all your bookmarked pages can take ages. Navigator adds a 'starburst' to the bookmark's icon if the page has been updated since your last visit; a question mark indicates that it couldn't reach the page.

Points of View
Welcome to PoliticsUSA
The Conservative Party
The Labour Party
THE LIBERAL DEMOCRATS
HotWired Network ————————— Unreachable page
FutureNet : .net - Index
Internet Magazine's Home Page ——————⟩ Updated pages
Women's Wire Home Page ——————
A Man's Life

Sorting Your Bookmarks

You can sort all your bookmarks into alphabetical order by selecting Sort Bookmarks from the Item menu of the Bookmarks window.

Sort is an all-or-nothing command which reorganises all your folders and all the bookmarks within them. If you're horrified by the result, select **Undo** from the **Edit** menu, or press **Ctrl+Z.**

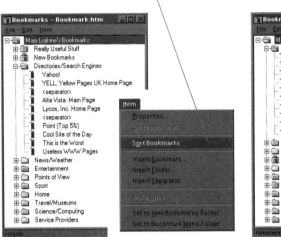

Bookmark Aliases (version 3 only)

An alias is like a Windows 95 shortcut; it's a copy of the bookmark that is updated automatically if the original is altered. Using aliases enables you to have the same bookmark in several folders.

You make an alias by clicking on a bookmark and selecting Make Alias from the Item menu. You can also right-click on the bookmark and select Make Alias from the pop-up menu. Aliases are displayed in italic text, but otherwise behave just like ordinary bookmarks – you can drag them from folder to folder or double-click to jump to the page.

Aliases

The Bookmark File

Your bookmarks are stored in a file on your hard disk; the default bookmark file is called bookmark.htm. If you want to share your bookmarks with a friend, or transfer them from home to work, all you have to do is copy this file. You'll find it in the directory you installed Navigator into.

You can have several bookmark files if you want, although one is enough for most people.

1 To create a second bookmark file, select Save As... from the File menu of the Bookmark window, or press Ctrl+S. This brings up the standard Windows Save As dialogue box. Give your bookmark file a new name and click Save.

2 You now have two identical bookmark files which you can edit and reorganise for different purposes. To switch from one to the other, select Open... from the File menu of the Bookmarks window (you can't have more than one bookmark file open at once).

HANDY TIP

HTML stands for HyperText Mark-up Language. Web page authors insert HTML 'tags' in their documents to tell Navigator how the pages should be displayed, where the links go to and so on. See page 89 for more details.

The bookmark file is an HTML document – it uses the same formatting codes as a Web page. This means you can display it in Navigator's main window.

3 Select Open File... from the File menu of the main Navigator Window, or press Ctrl+O. Find the bookmark.htm file and click Open. Your bookmarks are displayed as a list of links.

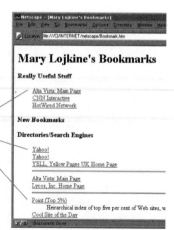

You might want to use your bookmark file as your Home page (see page 27). Copy its address, which will begin with `file:///`, from the Location bar.

Importing Bookmarks

It's easy to combine bookmark files – you simply import one into the other. You can also use the Import command to turn a page of links into a list of bookmarks.

1 To import one bookmark file into another, open the Bookmarks window, pull down the File menu and select Import.... This brings up an Open File-style dialogue box. Find the file you want to add to the current one and click Open.

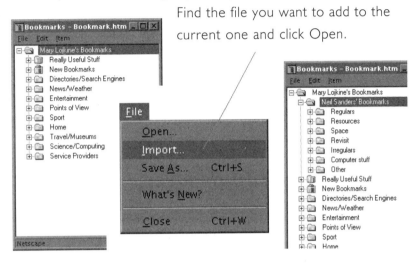

HANDY TIP

Importing a Web page only produces valid bookmarks if the page uses standard links. This technique doesn't usually work with pages from Web directories.

2 To turn all the links from Planet Science's Technology Hotspots page (see page 56) into bookmarks, first save the page onto your hard disk (see page 28). You can then follow the instructions from Step 1 to import the file. You will get a few odd entries, but it's easy to delete them.

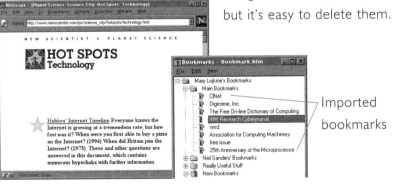

Imported bookmarks

Internet Shortcuts

Windows 95 users can create Internet shortcuts – desktop icons that enable you to open Netscape and go straight to a particular page. You can create as many as you want, so you could have shortcuts for all the pages you visit often.

1 To create a shortcut for the PA News Centre (see page 41), right-click on the page and select Internet Shortcut from the pop-up menu.

2 Check the Description, and edit it if necessary, then click OK.

3 An Internet shortcut icon will appear on your Desktop. Double-clicking on it runs Navigator, which prompts you to log on (if necessary), then takes you to the specified page.

There are three other ways to create Internet shortcuts:

1 Drag the link icon ![icon] (version 3 only) onto the Desktop. This method bypasses the Create... dialogue box.

2 Open the Bookmarks window and right-click on a bookmark, or drag it to the Desktop.

3 Right-click on a link, or drag it to the Desktop, to create a shortcut for the page at the other end.

CHAPTER SIX

Helper Applications

Helper applications extend Navigator's capabilities, enabling you to play sounds and videos, open Adobe PDF documents and decompress archived programs.

Covers

Helper Applications Explained 72

Setting up Helper Applications 73

Audio 74

Video 75

RTF and PDF Files 76

PostScript Files 77

Executable Files (Programs) 78

Compressed Files 79

Viruses 80

Helper Applications Explained

Navigator 2 can open text and image files and play some sound files; Navigator 3 can play most sound files and some videos. If you want to examine any other type of data file, you'll need a helper application.

World Wide Web pages sometimes include links to material that Navigator can't display, such as video clips (version 2) or specially formatted documents and program files (all versions). When Navigator encounters a data file that it can't deal with, it asks you whether you want to transfer the data to a more suitable application, such as a video player. You can also save the data file onto your hard disk and deal with it later, or cancel the transfer.

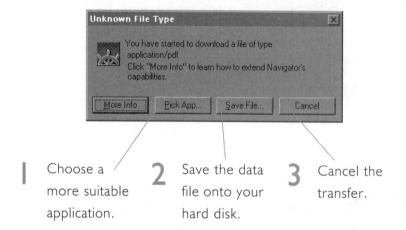

1 Choose a more suitable application.

2 Save the data file onto your hard disk.

3 Cancel the transfer.

The application that you transfer the data file to is called a 'helper application', or helper. You can speed things up by configuring Navigator to send particular types of files to particular applications automatically.

Unlike plug-ins (see Chapter Ten), helper applications are separate programs. Once Navigator has transferred the data, it has nothing more to do with the downloaded file – you use the helper's controls to play the sound or video, or view the document. When you're finished, you close the helper and return to Navigator.

Saving Files

If you opt to save the file instead, Navigator brings up the standard Windows Save As dialogue box, enabling you to choose a suitable folder (directory). The Saving Location dialogue box then appears, enabling you to monitor the download. Large files can take 20-30 minutes to download.

Setting up Helper Applications

You can tell Navigator to use a particular helper application every time it encounters a particular type of file. For example, you might tell it to transfer PDF files (see page 76) to Adobe's Acrobat Reader program.

1 Select General Preferences... from the Options menu and click on the Helpers tab.

You may find it easier to ignore the File type list and simply look for the correct extension – the three-letter tag which tells you what kind of file you're dealing with – in the right-hand list. (Windows 95 sometimes doesn't show file extensions. Turn them on by running Explorer, selecting Options... from the View menu and unchecking the Hide MS-DOS file extensions... box.)

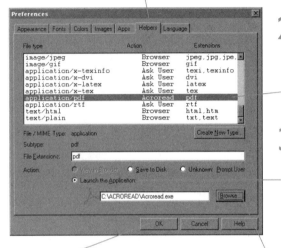

2 Scroll down the list of file types and click on application/pdf.

3 In the Action: section, click the Launch the Application: radio button.

5 Click OK to save the change and finish.

4 Click the Browse button to bring up a dialogue box which enables you to find the appropriate program file – in this case, acroread.exe.

Don't be put off by the length of the File type list – many of the entries are for users of the UNIX and Apple Mac versions. Apart from the various audio and video file types, the only ones you're likely to need are:

File Type	Type of Data	See Page
application/postscript	drawing	77
application/octet-stream	program	78
application/x-zip-compressed	archive	79
application/rtf	formatted text	76
application/pdf	formatted document	76

Audio

Navigator recognises three types of audio file: Windows wave (wav extension); Apple Macintosh aiff (aif, aiff and aifc) and basic audio files (au and snd). You're most likely to encounter .wav and .au files, and as long as you have a properly configured soundcard, you shouldn't have any problems playing them.

1 Navigator 2 has a built-in audio player which pops up when you download a basic audio or aiff file. It plays these sound samples automatically.

HANDY TIP

Media Player is part of Windows. It should be in your Windows directory.

2 You can use Media Player as a helper application for .wav files. Follow the instructions on page 73, selecting audio/x-wav as the file type and mplayer.exe as the application.

3 Navigator 3 has an audio plug-in, enabling it to play all three types of audio file. A tapedeck-style player appears within the window; click on the Stop, Play and Pause buttons to control the playback. You can also use the Volume slider to increase or decrease the volume.

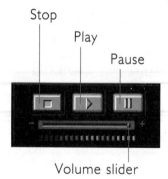

Stop

Play

Pause

Volume slider

Video

Video clips are fun, but the files are quite large and they can take a long time to download.

Navigator also recognises three types of video files: Video for Windows (avi extension); Apple Macintosh QuickTime (qt and mov); and mpeg video files (mpeg, mpg and mpe). Navigator 2 requires helper applications for all three types; version 3 can play .avi files, but requires helpers or plug-ins for QuickTime and mpeg video clips.

You will often find a selection of video players on the CD-ROMs that are given away with computer magazines. Installing a player from one of these discs is much easier than downloading one from the Internet.

1   You can use the Windows 95 version of Media Player to play avi files, such as this clip from NASA's Web site (see page 56). Follow the instructions on page 73, selecting video/x-msvideo as the file type and mplayer.exe as the application. If you have Windows 3.1, you'll need Microsoft Video for Windows.

You can only play QuickTime movies which have been saved in a PC-compatible format, so opt for the .avi version if you get a choice. Otherwise you may spend ages downloading a file, only to find that it won't play.

2   You'll need QuickTime for Windows to play QuickTime files, such as this Disney clip (see page 47). Select video/quicktime as the file type, click the Launch the Application radio button and locate the player.exe file.

3   Mpeg video files aren't as common as avi and QuickTime movies. There are a number of shareware mpeg players; if you can't find one on a disc, use one of the search engines (see page 39) to find a player on the Internet. Select video/mpeg as the file type and locate your player's .exe file.

RTF and PDF Files

Rich Text Format (RTF) Files

RTF files are formatted text documents. When you load one into your word processor, it'll look much the same as the original – the author's fonts (where possible), character and paragraph styles and document structure are preserved.

Most word processors – including Windows 95's WordPad – will open RTF files. Follow the instructions on page 73 to automate this, selecting application/rtf as the file type and wordpad.exe – or your word processor – as the application.

Portable Document Format (PDF) Files

PDF files contain laid-out documents, sometimes with illustrations. For example, many of the Virtual Garden (see page 53) project sheets are available as PDF files. You can view and print them using Adobe's Acrobat Reader.

You can download the Acrobat Reader from Adobe's Web site, at: http://www.adobe.com/ Follow the instructions on page 73 to use it as a helper application.

HANDY TIP

TimesFax (see page 42) is a PDF mini-edition of the New York Times. Adobe also maintains a list of Web sites with interesting or useful PDF files.

PostScript Files

HANDY TIP

PostScript files aren't as flexible or user-friendly as PDF files, which may eventually replace them on the Web. In the meantime, avoid them if you can – they're often more trouble than they're worth.

PostScript is a page description language: it tells PostScript printers how to 'draw' all the items on a page. Most of the PostScript files on the Web contain diagrams or illustrations.

Encapsulated Postscript files (eps extension) can be imported into most drawing and DTP packages, enabling you to view or print them. It's probably best to save them to disk and deal with them once you've logged off.

Regular PostScript files (ps extension) can be downloaded to a PostScript printer (if you aren't sure whether your printer supports PostScript, it probably doesn't). Alternatively, you can view and print them using a program which can interpret PostScript commands, such as Ghostscript. You can find out more about this program, and download all the necessary software, from the Ghostscript Web page, at:
`http://www.cs.wisc.edu/~ghost/index.html`

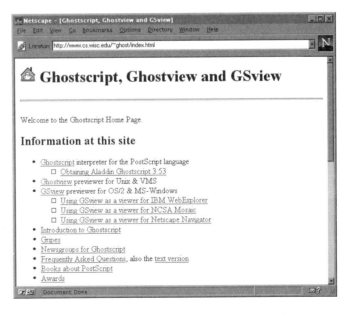

The Ghostscript Web page also explains how to use Ghostscript as a helper application.

Executable Files (Programs)

There's always a chance that a downloaded program might contain a virus. See page 80 for details.

Executable files (exe extension) are programs that you can run on your computer. Somewhat confusingly, their file type is application/octet-stream.

You can't load a program into another program, so there aren't any helper applications for executable files. Once you have selected application/octet-stream from the File type list, you have two choices:

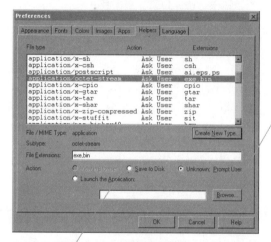

1 Leave Action: set to Unknown: Prompt User. You'll continue seeing the Unknown File Type dialogue box (see page 72) when you try to download a program. You'll then have to click the Save File... button to download the file onto your hard disk.

2 Change the Action: setting to Save to Disk to automatically save program files onto your hard disk. The standard Windows Save As... dialogue box will appear when you try to download a program, enabling you to select an appropriate folder (directory).

Compressed Files

Web page authors often use compression programs to 'archive' the program files linked to their pages. There are two reasons for this:

1 Most programs consist of several files – there may be a setup utility and help files as well as one or more .exe files. Creating an archive keeps them all together.

2 The resulting archive is often substantially smaller than the original group of files, so it downloads more quickly.

The most popular compression program on the PC, PKZIP, produces archives with a .zip extension.

You'll also come across self-extracting archives – these have an .exe extension and unzip themselves when you run them. For example, Netscape distributes Navigator as a self-extracting archive.

Once you have downloaded a .zip file, you'll need to decompress or 'unzip' it. There are numerous shareware unzippers, but PKZIP for Windows is probably the best choice for beginners. Get a copy from a shareware library or magazine cover disk, or download it from PKWARE's Web site at:
`http://www.pkware.com/`

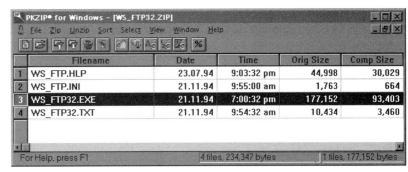

	Filename	Date	Time	Orig Size	Comp Size
1	WS_FTP.HLP	23.07.94	9:03:32 pm	44,998	30,029
2	WS_FTP.INI	21.11.94	9:55:00 am	1,763	664
3	WS_FTP32.EXE	21.11.94	7:00:32 pm	177,152	93,403
4	WS_FTP32.TXT	21.11.94	9:54:32 am	10,434	3,460

For Help, press F1   4 files, 234,347 bytes   1 files, 177,152 bytes

You can use PKZIP for Windows as a helper application, but it's better to save the .zip file onto your hard disk and decompress it when you're off-line. Select the file type application/x-zip-compressed and follow the instructions from step 2, opposite, to save .zip files automatically.

Viruses

If you're going to download programs from the Internet, you should invest in some antivirus software – preferably the sort which examines everything which is saved onto your hard disk. It's also a good idea to have a regular schedule for backing up any files that contain important information, or would be difficult to replace. The Internet isn't the seething cesspit of malicious code that it's sometimes made out to be, but it's certainly possible to pick up something nasty.

Broadly speaking, you can only get a virus if you download and run an infected program. As well as checking all the programs you download, you should also be wary of programs attached to e-mails or Web pages, binary files posted to newsgroups (see Chapter Thirteen) and documents which may contain macros – particularly Microsoft Word documents. Download files from large, well-managed file archives (see Chapter Eleven) or directly from the company concerned, and be very suspicious of anything sent to you by a stranger.

That said, you shouldn't throw away your modem or lie awake worrying about virus attacks. If you make backups, run antivirus software and exercise a modicum of caution, you're unlikely to get an infection you can't recover from.

CHAPTER SEVEN

Intermediate Web Browsing

By now you know more than enough to make use of the Web, and you've probably spent some time exploring it. This chapter covers additional features that help you find what you're looking for, move about more efficiently, get help with any problems you may have and learn something about the pages you've been looking at.

Covers

Finding Text 82

Reloading a Web Page 83

The History Window 84

New Windows 85

Directory Menu 86

Help Menu 87

Viewing HTML Codes 89

Document Information 90

Finding Text

The Find command enables you to check whether a Web page contains a particular word or phrase, and jump straight to it. It's useful when a search engine has taken you to a long page – rather than scrolling through it, you can use Find to locate the relevant section.

1. To search for a word or phrase, click on the Find button, select Find... from the Edit menu or press Ctrl+F.

2. Enter a word or phrase in the Find dialogue box and click the Find Next button.

See page 56 for details of NASA's extensive Web site.

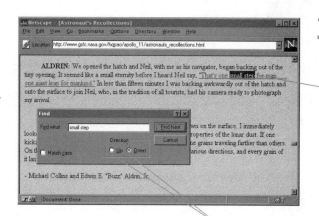

3. Navigator finds and highlights the text.

4. Click Find Next again to see if the text appears a second time, or enter a new word or phrase.

5. If the search text appears more than once, you can use the Up and Down radio buttons to go back to earlier occurrences or on to later ones.

Reloading a Web Page

Sometimes a page doesn't get downloaded properly, either because of problems on Internet, or (more often) because you've clicked on a link while the page was still downloading. If you then click the Back button, you'll find you only have half the page. You can get the rest back by pressing the Reload button.

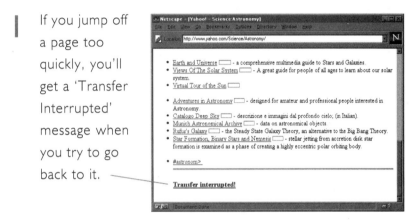

1 If you jump off a page too quickly, you'll get a 'Transfer Interrupted' message when you try to go back to it.

You'll also find a Refresh command on the View menu. Refresh redisplays the page using the data in your computer's memory, whereas Reload goes back to the original computer and checks whether the page has changed.

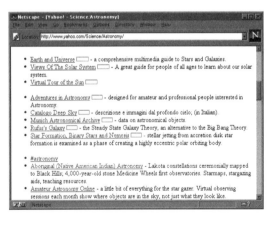

2 Click the Reload button, select Reload from the View menu or press Ctrl+R to download the rest of the page.

You can also use the Reload button to see the latest version of a page or image which is updated regularly. For example, some of NASA's pages are updated every minute or so if the space shuttle is in orbit.

The History Window

The History window displays a list of the pages you have visited recently. To some extent it duplicates the list at the bottom of the Go menu, but it provides more information and also enables you to make bookmarks.

1 To open the History window, select History from the Window menu, or press Ctrl+H.

2 The pages you have visited are listed in reverse order (most recent at the top), with the title on the left and the address (URL) on the right.

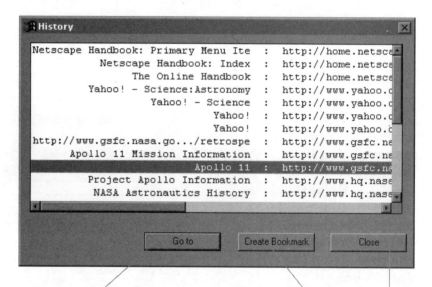

3 To return to a page, select it and click the Go to button, or double-click on its entry.

4 To bookmark a page, select it and click the Create Bookmark button.

5 You can leave the History window open alongside the main window as you browse, or press the Close button to clear it off the screen.

New Windows

Navigator allows you to have more than one main window open at once. For example, you might read an article in one window while you wait for an image-heavy page to download into another.

1 To open a second window, select New Web Browser from the File menu, or press Ctrl+N. The new window automatically displays the oldest page in your History list.

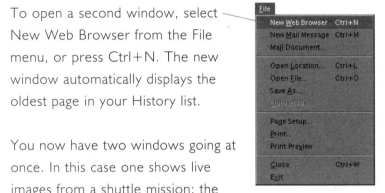

HANDY TIP

You can even have two or more pages downloading at once, although they'll download more slowly. See page 106 for more information.

2 You now have two windows going at once. In this case one shows live images from a shuttle mission; the other shows details of the payload.

HANDY TIP

See page 56 for details of NASA's extensive Web site.

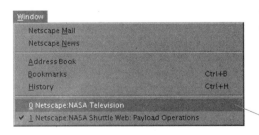

3 You can switch from one to the other by pulling down the Window menu and selecting the appropriate page title.

Directory Menu

The Directory menu is essentially a built-in bookmarks list. The items take you to pages on Netscape's Web site.

1 Takes you to the main page of the Netscape site.

2 Links to new Web pages which you might find interesting, complete with descriptions.

> Directory
>
> Netscape's Home
> What's New?
> What's Cool?

3 A list of sites deemed eye-catching, impressive, amusing, useful or just 'cool' by the people at Netscape.

4 Showcase for Netscape customers who have created innovative Web sites. You can also view some case studies.

5, 6 Pages which enable you to sample several search engines and directories.

> Netscape Galleria
> Internet Directory
> Internet Search
> Internet White Pages
> About the Internet

7 Links to services which help you find e-mail addresses and Web pages for people you know.

8 A few links to sites which provide information about the Internet and its services.

You can use the Directory buttons to access some of these items. Clicking on the Netscape logo at the right-hand end of the location bar takes you to Netscape's Home page.

| What's New? | What's Cool? | Handbook | Net Search | Net Directory | Software |

Help Menu

The items on the Help menu take you to Web pages which provide more information about Navigator and help you resolve any problems you have.

1. Find out which version you are using, and view the licence. You don't have to be on-line to load this page.

2. Find out which plug-ins (see Chapter Ten) are installed, or jump to the main plug-in information page.

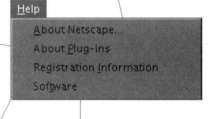

 UK users can purchase Navigator from Unipalm PIPEX – see pages 15 and 20 for more details.

3. Check your registration details, or register your copy of Navigator.

4. Register your copy and download upgrades or extra components.

Reference Section

The second section of the Help menu links you to the Handbook and various other problem-solving resources. You can use these pages to find out about any features added to Navigator since the publication of this book.

5. An indexed guide to all Navigator's features, complete with a tutorial and an introduction to the Internet.

6. Information about features specific to your version of Navigator.

7. A list of common questions – and their answers.

8. Information about Navigator's security features – see page 107.

...contd

REMEMBER

You can only access the Handbook while you're on-line.

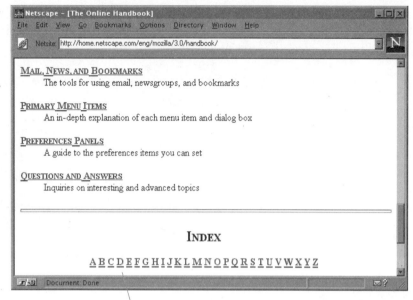

You can use the A–Z index at the bottom of the Handbook's main page to find a particular command quickly.

Feedback and Support

The third section of the Help menu enables you to communicate with Netscape. You can also find out about HTML, the language used to create Web pages.

9 Report any bugs or problems. This is particularly relevant if you've downloaded a pre-release or 'beta' version.

10 Ask Netscape for help. You're only entitled to e-mail support if you've purchased your copy of Navigator within the last 90 days.

11 Find out how to create your own Web pages.

Viewing HTML Codes

Web pages are created using HyperText Mark-up Language, generally shortened to HTML. It's a two-step process: you write your text, then you insert HTML 'tags'. These tags tell Navigator – or any other Web browser – how the text should be displayed, where to put the pictures and so on. Navigator doesn't normally display these tags, but you can force it to do so if you're curious about HTML.

1   To see what the front page of the Science Museum Web site (see page 55) 'really' looks like...

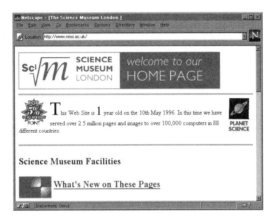

2   ...pull down the View menu and select Document Source. You can recognise the HTML tags because they are always surrounded by angled brackets < >.

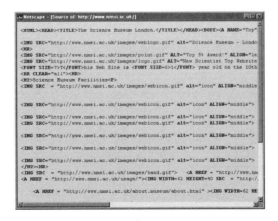

Document Information

You can use the Document Info window to find out when a page was last modified. You also get a list of all the pages, graphics and other items linked to it.

To open the Document Info window, pull down the View menu and select Document Information.

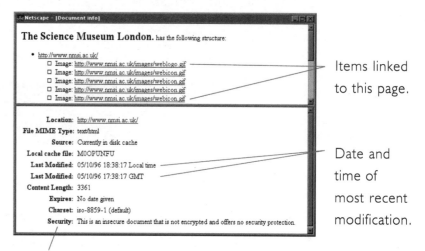

Items linked to this page.

Date and time of most recent modification.

Security status of the document – see page 107.

CHAPTER EIGHT

Interactive Web Pages

This chapter covers some of the ways that Web pages can be more than just a facsimile of a magazine or book page. Interactive elements, such as forms and animations, can make a page more useful, or just more fun to browse.

Covers

Forms 92

Site Registration 93

Web Chat 94

Frames 95

Client-Pull Page Updates 97

Server-Push Animation 98

Java 99

JavaScript 100

Forms

If you've explored some of the sites listed in Chapter Four, you've probably already encountered forms, either while entering keywords into a search engine, or while registering for one of the sites that keeps tabs on its users.

Entering data into a form is just like using a dialogue box – you either fill in the blanks or select preset options using drop-down lists, radio buttons or check boxes. Once you're done, you click the Submit button to send the data back to the host computer. Generally you'll get a response, in the form of another Web page, in a few seconds. For example, the Virtual Garden plant search page (see page 53) returns a list of plants that meet your criteria.

HANDY TIP

Check boxes allow you to select several options at once, whereas radio buttons only allow you to select one. Radio buttons are used for mutually exclusive options, such as 'male' and 'female'.

Text box

Drop-down list

Check boxes

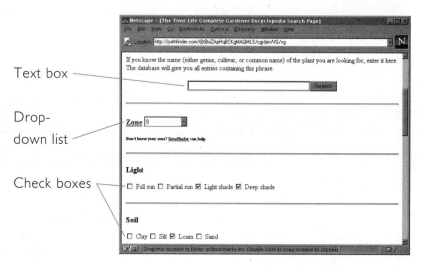

Forms aren't always dry and serious; they are often used for interactive gadgets such as humorous questionnaires and automatic letter writers.

Site Registration

Many of the large commercial sites require you to register for access. This isn't as sinister as it sounds – usually the company concerned just wants to find out what kind of people use the site so it can sell advertising. While it's hard to get excited about the prospect of ads on Web pages, they do help fund services that you might otherwise have to pay for, such as the Electronic Telegraph (see page 41).

Don't ever use your log-on name and password, as supplied by your service provider, for site registration. Anyone who knows these details can use your Internet account, so keep them secret.

Registration involves filling in a form and selecting a user name and password. Unless you're feeling very paranoid, or planning to make credit card purchases over the Web, you can use the same user name and password for several sites. They really only serve to identify you, rather than to provide security. Usually you won't even have to remember them – you simply bookmark the page after the registration page – but it's a good idea to write them down just in case.

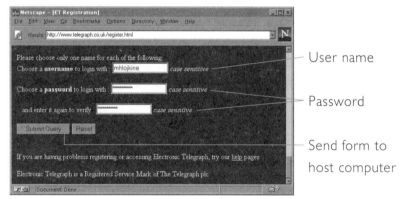

— User name

— Password

— Send form to host computer

There are some sites which you can only get access to by paying a regular subscription, usually by credit card. Often you can find an equivalent site which doesn't charge for access, so have a good browse around the Web before you commit yourself. If you're signing up for pay services, use a different password for each one, and keep those passwords secret.

Web Chat

Chat sites enable you to have a conversation – of sorts – with other Web users. It's more like passing notes in class than talking to someone face-to-face, though.

Chat pages have a form section at the top, where you enter your message, and a message area at the bottom, where the most recent messages are displayed. To join in, you simply type in a message and click the Send or Submit button. A few seconds later, your message is added to the bottom section, usually at the top.

Some pages update automatically; others require you to click the Reload button to see your contribution. More sophisticated sites use Java applets (see page 99) rather than forms, but the basic principles are the same.

With luck, someone responds to your message, you respond to theirs, someone else joins in... and you have a proper conversation. In practice, though, chat pages can be frustratingly slow and the messages correspondingly banal.

If you want to have a go, the Computers and Internet/ Internet/World Wide Web/Communication section of Yahoo! (see page 38) has links to lots of chat pages.

Frames

Frames divide a Web page into several sections that can be scrolled or updated separately. It's a bit like having two or more separate pages squashed into the main window.

Clicking on a link can change the contents of the current frame, or one of the other frames, or take you to a completely separate Web page. Frames are often used for menus, mastheads and copyright notices.

For example, *People* magazine's Movie Reviews Database uses three frames. The top one has links to the site's interactive section and main page; the left-hand frame contains the index; and the reviews appear in the right-hand frame. Clicking on one of the letters at the top of the left-hand frame brings the appropriate section of the index into the bottom of that frame; clicking on a film name brings the review into the right-hand frame.

You can find *People* magazine's Movie Review Database at:
`http://pathfinder.com/people/movie_reviews/`

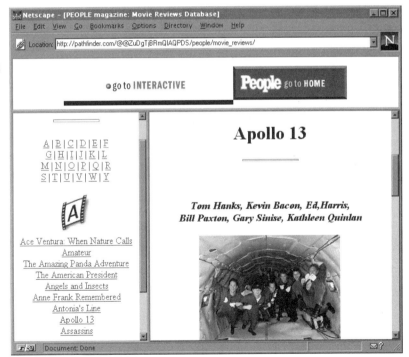

Browsing a page with frames is a bit different from browsing a regular page, because some commands only affect the selected frame.

1   To select a frame, click in it. If you look closely, you'll find that the selected frame has a grey border.

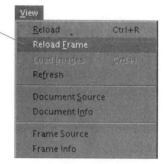

2   Sometimes you can adjust the size of a frame by using the mouse to drag the dividing bar. If the mouse cursor changes to two parallel lines with little arrows each side when you point at a bar, you can move it. If it doesn't, you're stuck with the frames as they are.

3   You can use the Reload Frame command (View menu) to reload just the selected frame. The regular Reload command (see page 83) updates all the frames on the page.

View	
Reload	Ctrl+R
Reload Frame	
Load Images	Ctrl+I
Refresh	
Document Source	
Document Info	
Frame Source	
Frame Info	

4   Other commands which only apply to the selected frame include Save As…, Print… and Load Images. If you want to see all the pictures, you must either load the images for each frame separately, or turn on Auto Load Images (see page 32) and reload the page.

5   In Navigator 3, the Back command (Go menu, or Back button) usually reverses the effect of your last action, no matter which frame is selected. In version 2, it takes you back to the previous complete page.

Client-Pull Page Updates

Sometimes you'll download a Web page, only to have it suddenly disappear and be replaced with another one. You haven't done anything wrong; the first page has used Navigator's 'client pull' capabilities to download the second page automatically.

 If you think you've been 'shunted' to a new address (normally the first page flashes onto the screen very briefly), it's a good idea to update any bookmarks which point to the old one.

Client pull is sometimes used to create welcome pages that stay on your screen for a few seconds, then give way to a menu page. It can also be used to redirect users when a site moves: you enter the old address, download a page with a client-pull directive and get shunted off to the new location automatically.

A Web author could conceivably create an automatic slideshow using client pull, but in practice most people let you move at your own pace. However, you will sometimes come across pages with data or images that are updated every minute or so.

You don't have to do anything to activate client pull – if a page includes a client-pull instruction, Navigator will go looking for the next page, whether you want it to or not. You can halt a client-pull download if you hit the Stop button at just the right moment, but the easiest way to escape a lengthy sequence is to go somewhere else. Use the Go menu to return to a 'normal' page, or select a bookmark from the Bookmark menu.

It can be a bit disturbing the first time you come across it, but client pull is almost always either useful or entertaining. If you'd like to see it in action, use one of the search engines (see page 39) to look for pages containing 'client pull' or 'client-pull'.

Server-Push Animation

Server push is the complement to client pull. In client pull the downloaded page requests or 'pulls' the new page; in server push the computer where the page is stored keeps sending or 'pushing' updates.

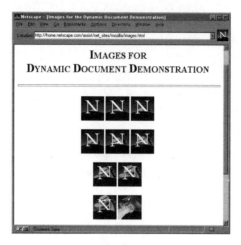

Server push is generally used to update images, creating a 'flipbook animation' effect. For example, Netscape's demonstration page uses ten images to create a brief animation in which the dragon (Mozilla, Netscape's mascot) appears to pop up from behind the logo and belch fire.

You may need to turn on Auto Load Images (see page 32) to see a server push animation. You don't have to do anything else to activate it – the sequence runs automatically. You can, however, interrupt a sequence by clicking on the Stop button, selecting Stop Loading from the Go menu, or pressing the Esc key.

Server push is often described as 'the poor man's animation', because the results are very jerky. Web page authors can create much smoother animations with Java (see opposite), so server push may eventually fall into disuse. In the meantime, though, you can locate lots of these animations by using a search engine (see page 39) to look for pages containing 'server push' or 'server-push'.

Java

Java is a programming language developed by Sun Microsystems. It enables Web authors to create small programs, or 'applets', which can be attached to Web pages. When you download the page, the applet is automatically downloaded and run.

Most versions of Navigator support Java – the exception is the Windows 3.1 version of Navigator 2.

 Java is also a type of coffee, so you'll find lots of coffee and caffeine puns on Java sites.

Java is often used to add animated images to Web pages, and to create small games. Scrolling messages are particularly popular, probably because they're easy to implement, but you'll also come across some neat graphical effects. It can also be used to create interfaces for Web chat (see page 94).

Unlike server-push animations, which arrive frame by frame, Java animations are downloaded completely before they are executed. Consequently they run smoothly, regardless of the speed of your connection, and can be a lot more sophisticated.

When you download a page with an attached applet, you'll see a blank rectangle, usually grey, in the area the applet uses. After a few seconds the rectangle is replaced by the animation or game (look out for an 'Applet Such-and-such running' message in the Status line). You don't have to start or stop the applet; you just watch or play, then move on to another page.

If you have version 3, you can tell Navigator not to run Java applets. You might want to do this if you have a slow connection and it's taking a long time for them to download. See overleaf for instructions.

JavaScript

JavaScript enables Web authors to create 'smart' pages that can respond to your actions without reconnecting to the server. For example, it can be used to create a clickable button which produces a message or new window, or to verify the information you've entered in a form. JavaScript is also used to place scrolling messages in the Status line.

From a user's point of view, the difference between Java and JavaScript is that Java programs are downloaded separately from the page they're attached to, whereas JavaScript commands are embedded in the page. This means that JavaScript effects are available as soon as the page appears on your screen, whereas Java applets often take 10–20 seconds to get going. Beyond that, they're both just tools for creating fancy effects.

Both Java and JavaScript were designed with security in mind, but it's possible that a malicious programmer could use them to attack your machine. If you have a lot of important files on your computer, you might want to turn off both features.

If you have Navigator 3, you can instruct it to ignore Java applets and/or JavaScript commands.

To turn off Java and/or JavaScript, go to the Languages section of Network Preferences and uncheck one or both check boxes.

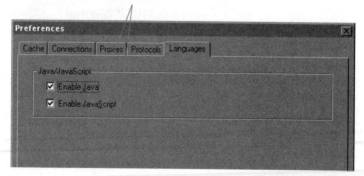

CHAPTER NINE

Advanced Configuration

Fine-tuning the Preferences settings customises Navigator to suit your way of working. This chapter covers the more important sections of the General, Network and Security Preferences dialogue boxes and discusses the difficult question of Internet security.

Covers

Appearance 102

Fonts 103

Colours 104

Cache 105

Connections and Proxies 106

Security 107

Appearance

HANDY TIP

The Images section of the General Preferences dialogue box is covered on page 36; Helpers is covered in Chapter Six. Mail and News Preferences are covered in Chapters Twelve and Thirteen respectively.

The Appearance section of the General Preferences dialogue box enables you to determine how the Toolbar and links are displayed. You can also decide what should happen when you first run the program.

1 Display pictures , text **Back** or both (default) on the Toolbar buttons. Picture- or text-only buttons take up less space.

2 Open the Web browser, mail and/or news sections of Navigator when you run the program.

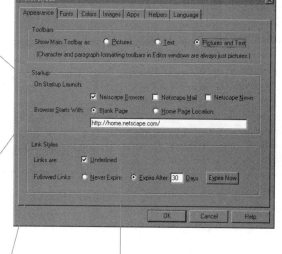

HANDY TIP

Click the Help button for a brief description of all the options. You don't have to be on-line to do this.

3 Start with a blank page, or go directly to the address in the text box (see page 27).

4 Display links in underlined (box checked) or plain (box unchecked) text.

5 Links change colour when you follow them, usually to purple (see page 104). Use this section to determine whether they stay that colour forever, or revert after a set number of days. Click on the Expire Now button to make all the links you've followed revert to their original colour.

Fonts

You can use the Fonts section of the General Preferences dialogue box to change the fonts used on Web pages. This is handy if you'd like the text to be a little larger, or just don't like Times New Roman.

The proportional font is used for most Web page text, and can be changed to anything you find easy to read.

The fixed-width font is sometimes used for paragraphs preformatted by the Web page author. It's also used for plain text documents, such as readme files, and text entered in forms and mail messages. It's best to stick with Courier New for your fixed-width font – choosing another font may spoil the layout of some pages.

| Unless you're browsing in a language that doesn't use the Latin alphabet, such as Japanese, leave this set to Latin1.

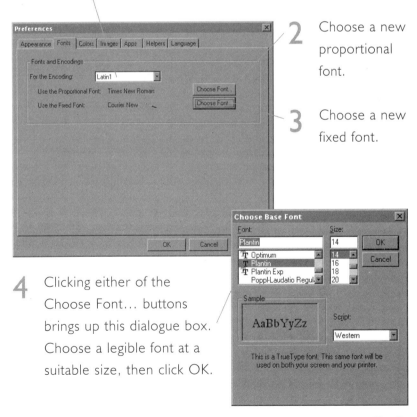

2 Choose a new proportional font.

3 Choose a new fixed font.

4 Clicking either of the Choose Font... buttons brings up this dialogue box. Choose a legible font at a suitable size, then click OK.

Colours

The Colors sections of the General Preferences dialogue box enables you to develop your own colour scheme.

HANDY TIP

If you often find yourself reading lengthy text documents on the screen, you might like to try white text on a navy background – it's easier on the eye.

1 Specify colours for links and regular text. Click on the Choose Color button to bring up the standard Windows colour selector.

2 Change the background colour of the main window.

3 Alternatively, you can display a picture behind the text. Click the Image File radio button, then click on Browse to locate a suitable file.

4 If you want Navigator to use your colours all the time, no matter what the author of the page has specified, check this box.

Once you've established a personal colour scheme, you can flip between it and the default scheme by checking and unchecking the Custom boxes – you don't have to reselect your colours each time.

Cache

REMEMBER

When you use the Reload button, Navigator checks to see if the page has been updated. If it has, it downloads it again; if it hasn't, it loads it from the cache. When you use the Back button, it doesn't bother checking, so you may get an out-of-date page. This really only matters if you're returning to a page which is updated every few minutes.

A cache is an area in memory, or on your hard disk, where the information you have downloaded can be stored temporarily. When you go back to a page you've looked at recently, Navigator tries to retrieve it from the cache rather than making you wait while it is downloaded again.

Navigator has two caches, one in memory and one on disk. The memory cache is cleared each time you close the program, but material in the disk cache is still available next time you run Navigator. Both are configured from the Cache section of the Network Preferences dialogue box.

The optimum sizes for the two caches depend on your computer and the way you use the Web. If you don't use the Back command much and rarely revisit sites, keep them small. Conversely, if you tread the same ground frequently, have plenty of memory and own a large hard drive, try allocating more space to both caches.

1 Allocate space to the two caches.

2 Disk cache directory (created automatically when you install Navigator).

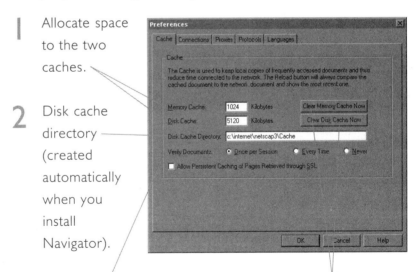

3 Verification: select Once... for optimum performance, or Every Time to always get the most up-to-date version of a page.

4 Use these buttons to clear the caches if you think there's a problem with their contents, or need to free up hard disk space.

Connections and Proxies

The Connections section of the Network Preferences dialogue box enables you to tell Navigator how many files to download at once.

Each time you download a page, an image on that page, a sound sample or any other file, Navigator has to establish a new connection to the server. You can have several connections open at once – the default is four. This means, for example, that you can go off and look at a few Web pages while you wait for a large file to download, because the pages are using separate connections from the file. It's like talking on the phone while you watch television, except all the data is coming down the same line.

However, your modem can only handle so much data at once, so the more connections you have, the slower each one will be. In practical terms, this means four is about the right number of connections – you won't speed things up by increasing this number, but you will have problems if you reduce it to one or two.

HANDY TIP

You may also need to use proxies if you are accessing the Web via a company network. Check with your systems manager.

Proxies

Some service providers store all the pages users have requested recently in a giant cache. Just as reloading a page from your disk cache is faster than downloading it again, accessing this cache is often faster than connecting to the original site, particularly if the Internet is busy.

The computer which holds the giant cache is called a proxy server, and you make use of this service by entering its details in the Proxies section of the Network Preferences dialogue box. Select Manual Proxy Configuration, then click on the View button and enter the details supplied by your service provider.

Security

Sooner or later everyone asks the same question: is it safe to send credit card details over the Internet? The short answer is that no one really knows. While it's technically possible for your transmission to be intercepted, the Web hasn't been in use long enough for anyone to be sure how likely it is that someone will take the trouble to do so.

It's a bit like giving your details over the phone, in that there are two things to worry about: is anyone listening in, and is the person on the other end genuine?

REMEMBER

Rather than creating secure sites, some companies require you to phone up with your credit card details. You still have to assure yourself that the company is genuine.

Navigator's built-in security features attempt to address both issues. Companies which wish to market products and services over the Internet can apply for a security certificate, enabling them to create secure servers which use encrypted forms. The system isn't infallible, but you can be reasonably confident that your details won't be intercepted, and that the recipient isn't an imposter.

There are several ways to identify a secure site: the URL will begin with https://; there will be a blue bar across the top of the main window; and the security logo in the lower left corner will be an unbroken key on a blue background.

 Secure document   Insecure document

For more information about the security status of a document, click on the key icon to bring up the Security dialogue box (version 3 only), or select Document Info from the View menu.

...contd

Most of the options in the Security Preferences dialogue box should be left at their default settings. However, you might like to turn off some of the warning messages and rely on your own common sense.

In particular, Navigator feels obliged to warn you every time you submit an unencrypted form to an insecure site. This can be very irritating, because often you couldn't care less whether anyone reads your message. If you're sending a comment to a chat site, for example (see page 94), the whole point is to make your views public.

Once you have turned off the insecure forms warning, it's up to you to check the security status of a site before you submit any sensitive information.

To turn off the warning about insecure forms, open the General section of the Security Preferences dialogue box and uncheck the Submitting a Form Insecurely option. ——

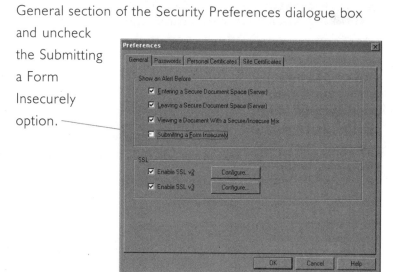

CHAPTER TEN

Plug-ins

Plug-ins enable you to add extra features to Navigator. This chapter explains how they work and introduces a few of the more interesting ones.

Covers

Plug-ins Explained 110

Installing Plug-ins 111

RealAudio 112

Shockwave...113

Acrobat 114

Live3D 115

EarthTime 116

Plug-ins Explained

Plug-ins are software add-ons that extend Navigator's capabilities. Unlike helper applications (see Chapter Six), they aren't stand-alone programs; they work with Navigator, enabling you to display multimedia presentations and formatted documents within the main window, play live audio and explore 3D worlds.

Most plug-ins are developed by companies other than Netscape, and new ones appear every month. For an up-to-date list, log on to Netscape's Plug-ins page.

To find out more about plug-ins, select About Plug-ins from the Help menu. Click on the 'click here' link to connect to Netscape's Web site (if you have version 2, select Software instead, then click on Download Components).

As the Web becomes more established, helper applications are gradually evolving into plug-ins, and some of the more successful plug-ins may eventually be incorporated into Navigator itself.

Installing Plug-ins

Most plug-ins are straightforward to install if you keep the following points in mind:

1. Make sure you download the right version. Most come in several 'flavours' – pick the one that's right for your computer and version of Navigator.

2. Read the instructions. Most sites provide step-by-step guides to installing their plug-ins; it's a good idea to print these out before you download the software.

3. You may run into problems if you have more than one copy of Navigator installed, so remove any old versions. Close Navigator before you try to install the plug-in.

4. Plug-ins are usually distributed as self-extracting archives (see page 79). Copy the .exe file into a temporary folder (directory), then run it. This will unpack the archive, and may also run the setup program. If it doesn't, look for a setup.exe file, and run it.

5. Follow the on-screen instructions to install the plug-in.

If you look at the Mime Type: entries you can usually guess which section corresponds to a particular plug-in.

6. To check whether the plug-in has been installed correctly, run Navigator and select About Plug-ins from the Help menu. You'll see a list of installed plug-ins.

RealAudio

RealAudio and Shockwave (see opposite) are the two 'must-have' plug-ins. Both are well supported, and they give you access to some of the most exciting sites on the Web.

RealAudio provides on-demand sound playback over 14,400 and 28,800bps connections. Sound samples in the RealAudio format are played as they are downloaded, rather than afterwards, so you start hearing sound a few seconds after you click on the link. RealAudio can also be used to 'Webcast' radio shows, news bulletins and live coverage of special events.

The control panel can be embedded in a Web page (above left) or displayed separately (above right). Sound quality deteriorates when the Internet is very busy, but generally it's acceptable, particularly for voice broadcasts. You can even leave the player running in the background while you use your computer for other tasks.

Find out more from the RealAudio Web site, at: http://www.realaudio.com/

Shockwave

Shockwave for Director enables you to view multimedia presentations created with Macromedia's Director authoring software. Director is often used for multimedia CD-ROMs, so there are lots of designers who know how to get the best out of it.

HANDY TIP

By now you'll have realised that there are lots of different ways to bring Web pages to life. Once you have all the right bits, you don't need to know how any of the effects are created, but having some idea about the various technologies enables you to interpret comments like 'this is a shocked site' or 'requires a Java-enabled browser'.

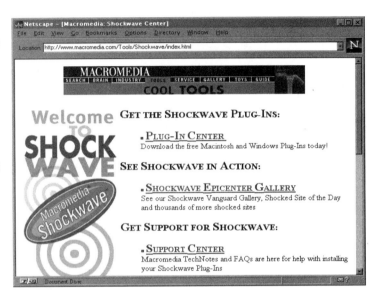

There are thousands of 'shocked' sites, and many of the presentations are very impressive. They can include text, graphics, animation, digital video, sound and interactive elements, and most don't take too long to download. There are even some Shockwave games.

If you're dubious about downloading plug-ins, Shockwave is a good one to start with – it's easy to install, and it really brings the Web to life.

You can find out more from Macromedia's Web site, at: http://www.macromedia.com/Tools/Shockwave/

Acrobat

Originally code-named 'Amber', version 3 of Acrobat Reader enables you to view Adobe PDF files (see page 76) in Navigator's main window.

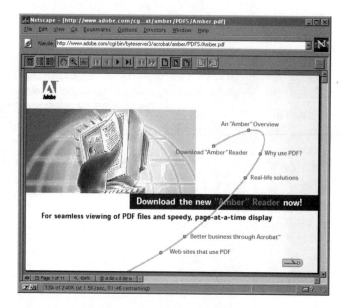

The plug-in adds its own toolbars across the top and bottom of the main window when you download a PDF document, enabling you to move from page to page or zoom in or out. It's much like using the previous version of Acrobat Reader, which ran as a helper application, except that everything happens within Navigator.

Integration with Navigator brings several benefits: PDF documents can include links to Web pages, as well as vice versa, and some documents can be viewed a page at a time (previously you had to download the whole file).

You can get more information from Adobe's Web site, at: `http://www.adobe.com/`

Live3D

Live3D is a Netscape plug-in that enables you to explore 3D objects and worlds. If it wasn't included with your copy of Navigator (it's bundled with some copies of version 3), you can download it from Netscape's site, at:
`http://home.netscape.com/`

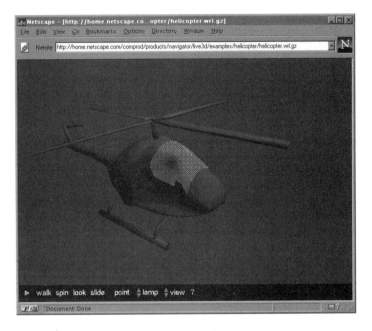

Live3D interprets objects created in VRML (Virtual Reality Modelling Language), enabling you to move around the virtual environment and view the objects from any angle. It takes a bit of getting used to, and the 'reality' is still very obviously virtual, but it's quite interesting to experiment with. Eventually we'll take 3D for granted, just as we now take it for granted that computers can display pictures.

EarthTime

Starfish Software's EarthTime is rather different from most plug-ins, in that it's an application rather than a viewer. It shows you the local time in up to eight cities around the world, calculates time differences and shows you which parts of the globe are in darkness.

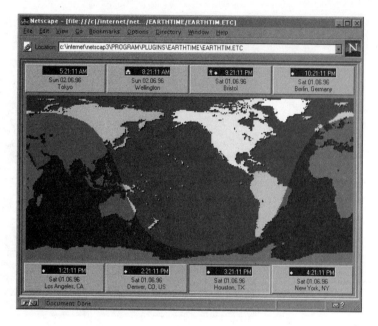

Most of its features – including the time displays – are accessible while you're off-line. In fact, you only need to log on if you want to synchronise your computer's clock with one of the Internet time servers.

To find out more, log on to Starfish Software's Web site, at: http://www.starfishsoftware.com/

CHAPTER ELEVEN

FTP and Gopher

As well as helping you to access the Web, Navigator enables you to make use of other Internet services, including FTP and gopher. This chapter explains how to download programs and documents from these sites.

Covers

FTP Explained 118

Connecting to FTP Sites 119

Downloading Files 120

Uploading Files 121

Useful FTP Sites 122

Gopher Explained 125

Connecting to Gopher Sites..126

FTP Explained

FTP stands for File Transfer Protocol, and it's a way of moving data from one computer to another. It isn't as popular as it used to be, mainly because the Web is more attractive and easier to use, but FTP sites are still used to store programs, documents and images. These sites are often referred to as 'archives', and you can think of them as the Internet equivalent of public libraries – except you don't have to return the files.

PD, Freeware and Shareware

Most of the software available from FTP sites is public domain, freeware or shareware. The first two can be used free of charge; the last is 'try before you buy' software. If you use a shareware program regularly, you have to pay a fee to the author. The fees are generally very reasonable and there is usually a reward for paying up or 'registering'. You might get a password which unlocks additional features, for example, or a printed manual. You'll find the details in the readme files associated with the program.

Basic Principles

Using an FTP site is much like locating a file on your hard drive – you simply work your way down through the folders (directories) until you find the file you're looking for. You can then download it to your computer. That's all there is to it, really – FTP doesn't have nearly as many bells and whistles as the Web.

Web pages occasionally link you directly to an FTP site, so it's handy to know how they work. If you want to spend a lot of time exploring FTP sites, you should get yourself a dedicated FTP program. Navigator is fine for downloading or uploading a few files every now and again, but it isn't as flexible as a specialist FTP program.

Connecting to FTP Sites

Connecting to an FTP site is just like connecting to a Web page – you simply enter the address in the Location bar or Open Location dialogue box. The only difference is that FTP addresses begin with `ftp://` rather than `http://`.

1 To connect to SunSITE at Imperial College (see page 122), select Open

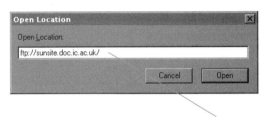

Location from the File menu (or press Ctrl+L), type its address into the dialogue box and click open.

The welcome message often contains important information about the site. You should also look out for readme files – click on the filename to display the text in the main window. You can ignore any instructions about typing in commands, though – these are for people with specialist FTP applications.

2 A welcome message and a list of files and folders appear in the main window.

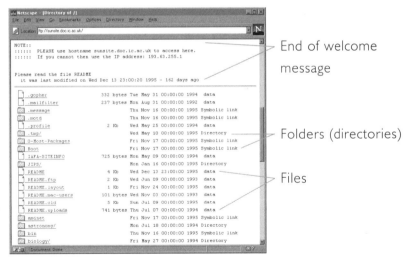

End of welcome message

Folders (directories)

Files

3 The files you can access will usually be a 'pub' folder – click on it to find out what it contains. Keep clicking on folders to move down the hierarchy. Use the Back button to work back up, or look for a Return... link at the top of the listing.

Downloading Files

HANDY TIP

The hardest part of using an FTP site is deciphering the filenames. Look out for index files, which usually contain brief descriptions of all the files in a folder. Click on the filename to display the index in the main window.

Once you've found your way into the right folder and located an interesting file, it's very easy to download it to your computer.

1 To download a file, simply click on it with the mouse.

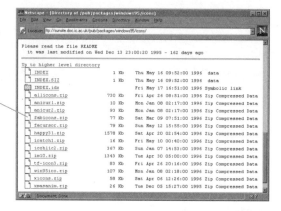

2 Unless you have configured Navigator to save files automatically (see pages 78–9), the Unknown File Type dialogue box will appear. Click Save File to bring up the standard Windows Save As... dialogue box.

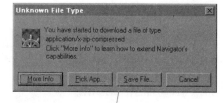

HANDY TIP

The speed of the download depends on the number of people using the Internet. The best time to download large files is first thing in the morning.

3 Once you've selected a folder and/or edited the filename, click the Save button to download the file. The Saving Location dialogue box pops up, enabling you to monitor the download. You can click the Cancel button if you decide you don't want the file after all.

Uploading Files

The incoming or uploads folder usually contains information about what you can upload and whom you should notify about the new file.

Some sites also allow you to upload files. If you're into computer art, for example, you might upload some of your pictures for other users to enjoy.

You generally upload your files into an 'incoming' or 'uploads' folder. The system manager can then check them out and move them to the appropriate location.

1 To upload a picture to SUNET (see page 122), connect to the site and work your way down to the pub/pictures/uploads folder.

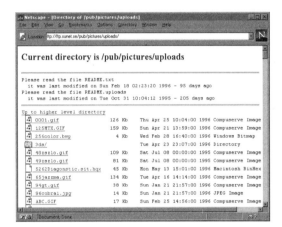

2 Select Upload File... from the File menu and locate the file. (You may need to change the Files of type: setting to All Files.)

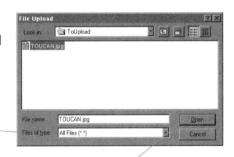

3 Click the Open button to start the upload.

4 Keep an eye on the Status line, which tells you how much of the file has been sent.

Useful FTP Sites

FTP addresses are usually written without the `ftp://`**. If you see an address like:** `ftp.funet.fi` **you must add the rest yourself, giving:** `ftp://` `ftp.funet.fi/`

SunSITE
ftp://sunsite.doc.ic.ac.uk/

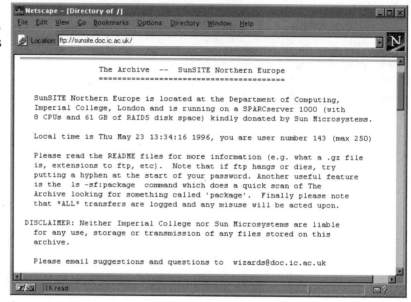

Many large FTP sites maintain up-to-date copies of sections of other sites. This is called 'mirroring', and it means you should be able to find most popular files on almost every large FTP site.

Based at Imperial College in London, SunSITE has space for over 60Gb of data. Unless you know exactly what you're looking for – and exactly where it is – it's best to start in the packages folder.

You could also try:

SUNET, a large user-friendly archive maintained by the Swedish University Network. Find it at: `ftp://ftp.sunet.se/`

Demon FTP, an archive maintained by the popular UK service provider. It isn't as vast as SunSITE, but you might find it easier to navigate. Start in the pub folder, then try ibmpc if you're looking for software. Find the site at: `ftp://ftp.demon.co.uk/`

Project Gutenberg
ftp://nptn.org/pub/e.texts/gutenberg/

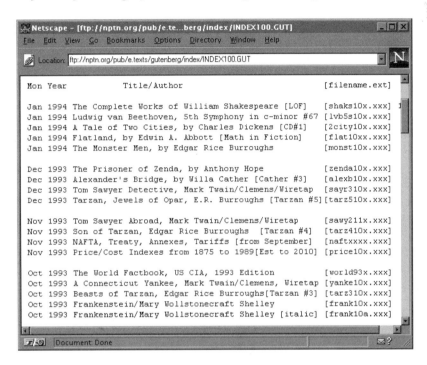

Project Gutenberg encourages people to create and distribute electronic versions of English-language texts. Most of the fiction dates back to last century, but you can also download electronic versions of reference works as diverse as The Complete Works of Shakespeare, The Bible, the first 100,000 prime numbers, Roget's Thesaurus, Abraham Lincoln's First Inaugural Address and The Communist Manifesto.

Smithsonian Photograph Collection
ftp://photo1.si.edu/

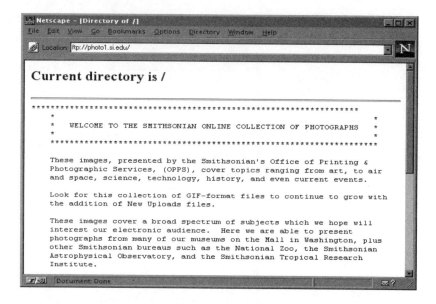

The Smithsonian's photograph collection covers art, science, technology, history and current events, and includes images from many of the museums on the Mall in Washington. The images are interesting and well scanned, and you're allowed to make use of them in non-commercial projects.

You could also try:

SUNET (see page 122) has lots of well-organised picture files, including many images from films and television programmes.

Gopher Explained

Gopher sites look much like FTP sites, but conceptually they have more in common with the Web, because they can give you access to files on several different computers. They use menus rather than folders, and generally provide access to reports and documents rather than program files.

This is one of the University of Tasmania's gopher menus (see overleaf). Selecting the second item…

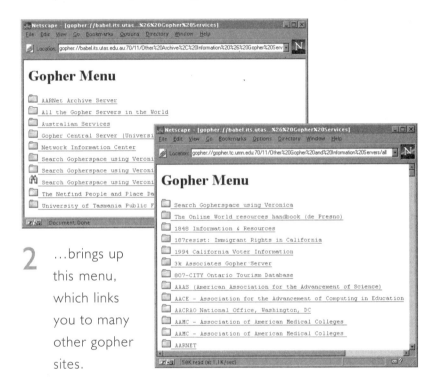

2 …brings up this menu, which links you to many other gopher sites.

Unless you actively hunt them down – and it's hard to think of a good reason why you should – you won't come across many gopher sites. They've been pretty much superseded by the Web, which does the same job in a more user-friendly fashion.

Connecting to Gopher Sites

REMEMBER

Like FTP addresses, gopher URLs are usually written without the `gopher://`**. You must add this prefix before you type the address into Navigator.**

Again, connecting to a gopher site is just like connecting to a Web page, except the address begins with `gopher://`.

1 To connect to the University of Tasmania's gopher site, select Open Location from the File menu, or press Ctrl+L, and type its address into the dialogue box.

HANDY TIP

You can bookmark FTP and gopher sites – simply select Add Bookmark from the Bookmark menu, or press Ctrl+D. You'll probably have to open the bookmark's Properties box (see page 63) and give it a sensible name.

2 The site's main menu appears in Navigator's main window. You can move to any sub-menu by clicking on it.

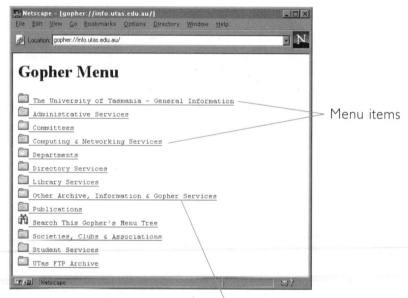

Menu items

3 Select the Other Archive... menu item to access the menus shown on the previous page.

CHAPTER TWELVE

Mail

Navigator's Mail feature enables you to send a message to anyone who is connected to the Internet.

Covers

E-mail Explained 128

Sending Mail 129

The Mail Window 131

Receiving Mail 133

On- and Off-line Mail 135

Attachments 136

The Address Book 138

Signature Files 140

E-mail Explained

Navigator's menus, dialogue boxes and on-line handbook refer to 'mail' rather than 'e-mail'. It's the same thing.

E-mail is short for electronic mail, and it's the Internet equivalent of letters and faxes. It's better than either, though, not only because it's quick and cheap, but also because you can attach files to an e-mail. This means you can send text documents, pictures, sound samples, program files and Web pages as well as simple messages.

You can send e-mail to anyone on the Internet; you just need to know their address, which will look something like:

mhl@dircon.co.uk

The part before the @ is the recipient's user name.

The part after the @ is the address of the recipient's service provider.

If you want to use Navigator to send and receive mail, you must fill in the Servers and Identity sections of the Mail and News Preferences dialogue box – see pages 18–19.

When you send a mail message, it is delivered to the recipient's service provider very quickly – usually within a few minutes. It is then stored in the recipient's mail box until he or she next logs on and checks for new mail.

E-mail is very efficient if you're dealing with someone who checks their mail regularly, but not so good for getting messages to people who only log on once a week. It's also very handy for contacting people who are perpetually on the phone or out of the office, and it makes it easier to deal with people in different time zones – rather than calling at an awkward hour, you can have a message waiting for them when they arrive at work.

Sending Mail

Many Web pages have special links which enable you to send mail to their authors. Look for an underlined name or e-mail address, a 'send mail' message or a picture of an envelope or postbox.

HANDY TIP

To find out more about the Planet Science Web site, turn to page 56.

1 If you hold the mouse pointer over one of these special links, you'll see an address beginning with mailto: in the Status bar.

2 To send a message, simply click on the link. The Message Composition window pops onto your screen.

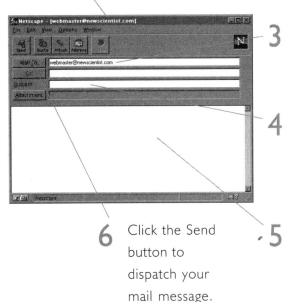

3 The address is entered automatically.

4 Enter a brief description of the contents of your message.

6 Click the Send button to dispatch your mail message.

5 Type your message into the main window.

...contd

As long as you know their e-mail addresses, you can also contact people who don't have Web sites.

1 Select New Mail Message from the File Menu, or press Ctrl+M.

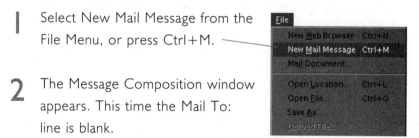

2 The Message Composition window appears. This time the Mail To: line is blank.

You can send mail to yourself – just enter your own address in the Mail To: box. This is handy when you're trying out the various options.

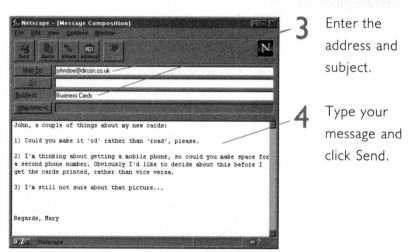

3 Enter the address and subject.

4 Type your message and click Send.

If you don't know someone's e-mail address, there's no easy way to find it – other than by asking them. You can try the on-line address books, sometimes referred to as 'White Pages' (see page 86), but they're by no means complete.

You can send the same message to several people at once by entering more than one address in the Mail To: box, or by adding additional recipients to the Cc: box.

The Mail Window

HANDY TIP

If you get tired of entering your password every time you check your mail, go to the Organisation section of the Mail and News Preferences dialogue box and turn on Remember Mail Password.

Although you can send mail from Netscape's main window, you must open the Mail window to receive messages. The Mail window enables you to read, reply to and/or file your mail, and also to compose new messages.

1 Pull down the Window menu and select Netscape Mail, or click on the envelope icon at the right-hand end of the status bar.

2 Enter your mail password. This may be different from your log-on password – check with your service provider.

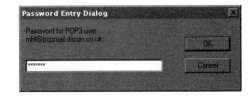

Mail Window Layout

The Mail window is divided into three sections:

Folders for incoming, pending, sent, deleted and filed messages – see overleaf.

Messages in selected folder (indicated by dotted line – currently the Inbox). New messages are highlighted with green flags and bold type.

HANDY TIP

You can adjust the relative sizes of the three areas by dragging the dividing bars with the mouse.

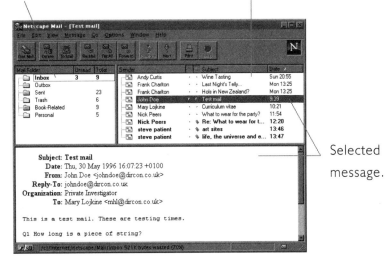

Selected message.

The top left-hand section of the Mail window contains up to four folders created by Navigator, plus any folders you create yourself. You won't see all four of the Navigator-generated folders the first time you open the Mail window, though – they're added as you need them.

New messages are placed in the Inbox.

The Outbox stores messages which are ready to send, but haven't actually been dispatched yet – see page 135.

HANDY TIP

If you don't want Navigator to copy messages to the Sent folder, go to the Composition section of Mail and News Preferences and delete the entry in the Mail File: text box.

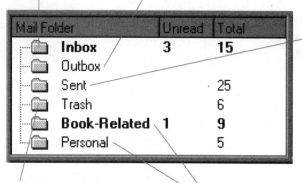

Mail Folder	Unread	Total
Inbox	**3**	**15**
Outbox		
Sent		25
Trash		6
Book-Related	**1**	**9**
Personal		5

Unless you tell Navigator otherwise, copies of all the messages you send are placed in the Sent folder.

The Trash folder contains messages which are ready to be deleted – see page 134.

You can create extra folders and file messages you might want to read again.

Folders which contain unread messages are highlighted with bold type.

Creating New Folders

Sometimes you'll want to file messages for future reference.

To create an extra folder, select Add Folder... from the Mail window's File menu and enter a suitable name.

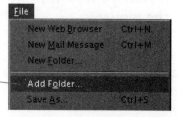

File	
New Web Browser	Ctrl+N
New Mail Message	Ctrl+M
New Folder...	
Add Folder...	
Save As...	Ctrl+S

Receiving Mail

Each time you open the Mail window, Navigator connects to your service provider's mail server and downloads any new messages. Incoming messages are automatically placed in the Inbox.

1 To read a message, click on it. The text is displayed in the bottom window; use the scroll bars to move though it.

2 The green flag is removed when you open a message, and the message title is displayed in plain

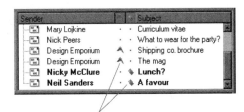

text. You can restore the green flag by clicking on the grey dot in front of the title, or mark an important message with a red flag by clicking on the other grey dot.

Replying to a Message

It's very easy to reply to a mail message, because Navigator adds the correct address automatically.

Whether or not the original message is quoted at the beginning of a reply depends on a setting in the Composition section of Mail and News Preferences. Uncheck the Automatically quote... box if you don't want the original quoted. You can still quote the message manually – see overleaf.

1 To reply to a message, open it, then click the Re: Mail button. Navigator opens a new Message Composition window.

2 The text of the original message is usually quoted at the top of the new one. Type your reply and click Send.

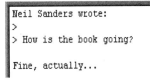

Forwarding Messages

You can also forward a mail message to a third party.

1 To forward a message to another friend or colleague, open it and click the Forward button. Enter the new address in the Mail To: box.

2 The message will appear to be blank; this is because the original is sent as an attachment (see page 136). Add any comments you wish to make, and click Send. The original message will be added at the bottom as the new one is sent.

3 Alternatively, follow the instructions in step 1, then select Include Original Text from the File menu, or click the Quote button, to copy the text into the new message. You must then detach the attachment. Click Attachment, then click Delete and OK.

Organising Your Mail

Once you've responded to a message, file or delete it.

HANDY TIP

You should clear out all your 'trashed' messages every few days. Select Empty Trash Folder from the File menu to delete them permanently.

1 To file a message, create an extra folder (see page 132) and drag the message across to it.

2 If you've finished with a message, drag it to the Trash folder, or select it and click the Delete button. This doesn't actually delete it – you can open the Trash folder and drag it out again if necessary.

On- and Off-line Mail

Working Off-line

You don't have to be on-line to compose messages. If you're concerned about your phone bill, log on, collect all your mail and log off again. You can then read and reply to the messages at your leisure. Once you've done this – and composed any new messages – log on and dispatch all your messages at once.

 Don't forget to send your messages! It's very easy to just transfer them to the Outbox and then forget all about them. You must also remember to reselect Immediate Delivery from the Options menu if you want to send a message while you're on-line.

1 When you're working off-line, select Deferred Delivery from the Options menu of the Message Composition window

before you click the Send button. This transfers the message to the Outbox rather than actually sending it.

2 When you log on again, select Send Mail in Outbox from the File menu, or press Ctrl+H, to dispatch your messages.

Working On-line

If you spend a lot of time on-line, you might want to instruct Navigator to check for mail at regular intervals.

In the Servers section of Mail and News Preferences, set Check for Mail: to Every: 10 or 15 minutes.

 If you see a question mark by the mail icon, Navigator needs your mail password. Open the Mail window and enter it to initiate automatic checking.

Navigator then checks for mail regularly. New mail is indicated by a change in the mail icon:

No new mail   New mail!

When you open the Mail window, Navigator downloads the new message(s).

Attachments

As well as sending simple text messages, you can mail pictures and document files to your friends and colleagues. This is handy if you're collaborating on a report, and can be a lot of fun, too.

BEWARE

Some e-mail packages don't support attached files, so if you're sending a message to someone who doesn't use Navigator, try to keep things simple.

1 To attach a file to your message, click Attach or Attachment to bring up the Attachments dialogue box.

2 Click Attach File... and locate the file or files you wish to attach, then click OK.

3 When you receive a message with an attached file, it will be displayed either as part of the message...

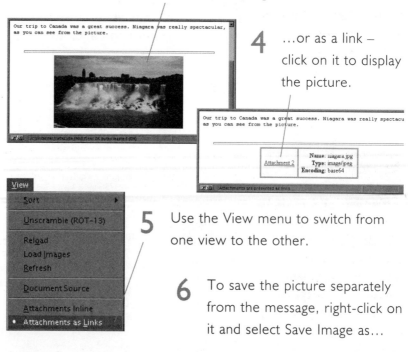

4 ...or as a link – click on it to display the picture.

5 Use the View menu to switch from one view to the other.

6 To save the picture separately from the message, right-click on it and select Save Image as...

...contd

Attaching Web Pages

You can even attach a Web page to a mail message. The text will appear exactly as it appears on the screen, along with a link to the page itself. The images aren't included, but your friend can download them from the original site.

You can also send just the text of the page, without the formatting instructions. This is handy if you're sending it to someone who doesn't use Navigator for e-mail. Click the Attachment: button and select Convert to Plain Text before you send the message.

1 To attach the page you're currently browsing to a new mail message, select Mail Document... from the File menu.

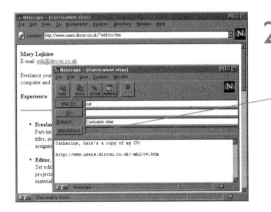

2 A new message is created, with the page already attached (check the Attachment line to make sure).

3 The page arrives with all its formatting intact. Click a link to download the appropriate page to Navigator's main

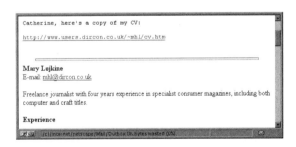

window, or select Load Images from the View menu to download the pictures.

You could just as well send your friend the address by itself, without bothering to include the page, but attaching it makes for a very impressive e-mail!

The Address Book

Just as the Bookmarks file stores the details of your favourite Web sites, the Address book stores your favourite e-mail addresses, saving you some typing and helping you to get them correct.

1 Select Address Book from the Window menu. At first the Address Book will be empty, but soon it will look very much like your Bookmarks list.

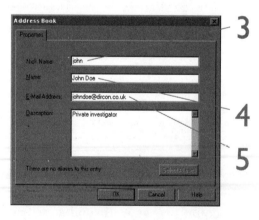

— User

Mailing lists, which enable you to mail several people simultaneously (see opposite).

HANDY TIP

If you receive a message from someone new, you can add them to your Address Book by opening the message and selecting Add to Address Book from the Message menu.

2 To add an address, select Add User from the Item menu.

3 Enter a short version of the person's name, all in lower case...

4 ... their full name...

5 ...and their address, then click OK (the description is optional).

6 To send a message to this person, open the Message Composition window and type their nickname in the Mail To: line. Alternatively, click on the Mail To: button to bring up a list of all the people in your Address book.

Mailing lists

A mailing list collects together a group of people that you might want to send the same message to simultaneously. Rather than entering all the names in the Mail To: line, you simply enter the name of the list.

Mailing lists are not like bookmark folders! When you select a bookmark folder, you are able to choose any of the bookmarks within it. When you select a mailing list, the message is automatically sent to everyone on that list. Many people have embarrassed themselves by accidentally sending a private message to all the people on a mailing list.

1 To create a new mailing list, select Add List from the Item menu and fill in the Properties box.

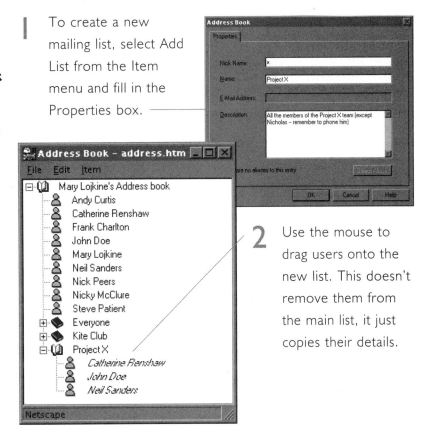

2 Use the mouse to drag users onto the new list. This doesn't remove them from the main list, it just copies their details.

Even if the people you know have nothing in common, an 'Everyone' list can be handy for notifying all your friends and colleagues of a change in address, forthcoming holiday or other special event.

Signature Files

Unless you only send messages to people you know well, it isn't a good idea to include your personal phone number or home address in your signature file.

A signature file is a short piece of text which is automatically appended to the end of every message you send. If you're sending messages from work, it might include your contact details; otherwise you could include a personal comment or favourite quote.

You can create a signature file in any word processor. Use Courier New, so you can see how it will look at the bottom of a mail message. Each line must contain no more than 79 characters, and end with a carriage return. Save it as a plain text file (txt extension).

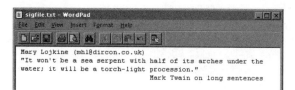

Once you've created a signature file...

2 ...go to the Identity section of Mail and News Preferences and tell Navigator where it is. Use the Browse button if you can't remember.

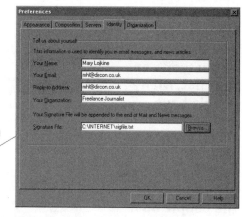

Keep your signature short – long ones get very tedious very quickly.

3 Your 'signature' will now be added to the end of all your messages.

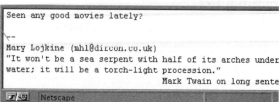

CHAPTER THIRTEEN

Newsgroups

Usenet newsgroups enable you to communicate with
Internet users who share your interests.

Covers

Newsgroups Explained 142

Getting Started 144

Subscribing to Newsgroups 145

Reading Messages 146

Posting Messages 147

Netiquette 148

FAQs 149

Smileys and Acronyms.. 150

Typical Newsgroups 151

Newsgroups Explained

The Usenet newsgroups are the Internet equivalent of your local pub or social club. They're nowhere near as pretty as the Web, but they're a good deal more interactive. If you're looking for gossip, trivia, advice, arguments and – very occasionally – news, Usenet is the place to find it.

Newsgroup 'messages' are also referred to as 'posts' and 'articles'. The three terms are interchangeable.

A newsgroup is essentially a public mailbox dedicated to a particular topic. Anyone on the Internet can post a message, and anyone else can read it and upload a reply.

Unlike a Web page, though, the 'mailbox' exists in more than one place. All the messages are regularly copied from one news server to another, enabling you to access them locally. Rather than connecting to lots of sites from all over the globe, you simply download the latest messages from your service provider's news server.

There are over 15,000 newsgroups to choose from. Some have a close-knit community of regular posters; others are larger and more anonymous. Either way, though, there's almost certain to be someone who wants to share your experiences, answer your questions, ask you for advice or just pass the time of day.

Understanding Newsgroup Names

Newsgroup addresses look like:
`rec.arts.movies.reviews`

or sometimes:
`news:rec.arts.movies.reviews`

Newsgroups are organised hierarchically: each section of the address (moving from left to right) reduces the scope of the group. In this case `rec` stands for recreation, `arts` and `movies` are self-evident and the group only carries `reviews`. There are ten other `movies` groups, about 100 other `arts` groups, and over 500 `rec` groups in total.

`rec` is only one of hundreds of top-level categories. Fortunately, you can find almost everything you want in just seven sections: `alt`, `comp`, `news`, `rec`, `sci`, `soc` and `uk`.

HANDY TIP

The alt. binaries **newsgroups contain** messages with attached files – pictures, sounds, extra levels for games and so on. Navigator doesn't always decode these attached files properly, so you're better off trying to find similar files on Web or FTP sites.

alt (alternative)

Almost anyone can create an alt newsgroup, so the alt hierarchy is one of the liveliest and busiest sections of Usenet. Some of the groups are pretty wild, but most are just odd – if you're interested in alien conspiracies, urban legends or breakfast cereal (no, really), alt has much to offer. It's also a nursery for new groups, some of which eventually graduate to the more respectable hierarchies.

comp (computing)

The comp groups cover everything from hardware and software to artificial intelligence and home automation.

news (Usenet)

The news groups cover Usenet itself, and are mostly unexciting. news.announce.newusers contains lots of information for beginners.

rec (recreation)

The rec groups covers hobbies, sports, arts and music, and are generally the best place to start. They tend to be friendlier than the alt groups and it's relatively easy to find your way around.

HANDY TIP

Turn to page 151 for brief descrip- tions of several typical newsgroups.

sci (science)

The sci groups cover mathematics, physics, engineering, chemistry, biological science, medicine, psychology and philosophy – everything except computing, basically.

soc (social)

The soc groups deal with social issues. The biggest subsection, soc.culture, has well over 100 groups dedicated to various countries and cultures. Genealogy, history and religion are also well represented, and there are a number of support groups.

uk (United Kingdom)

The uk groups are a microcosm of Usenet as a whole. The most popular groups are uk.politics and uk.misc, but you'll also find job ads, an *Archers* group and a selection of rec and religion groups.

Getting Started

If you want to use Navigator to access Usenet news, you must fill in the Servers and Identity sections of the Mail and News Preferences dialogue box – see pages 18–19.

Just as you must open the Mail window to receive messages, you use the News window to access newsgroups.

1 To open the News window, select Netscape News from the Window menu.

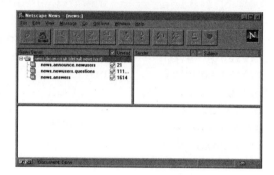

There isn't much to see at first – just three newsgroups in the top left-hand window. You need to download the newsgroup list from your service provider's news server.

2 Select Show All Newsgroups from the Options menu, then click OK. It takes 5–10 minutes to download the complete list.

3 The list appears in the top left-hand window. The groups appear in alphabetical order, and folders are used to display the hierarchies neatly.

Some service providers don't carry all the newsgroups. If there's something you particularly want, try asking if it can be added to their list.

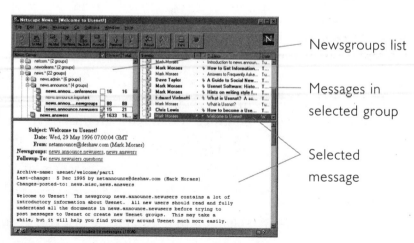

— Newsgroups list

— Messages in selected group

— Selected message

Subscribing to Newsgroups

Subscribing to a newsgroup isn't like subscribing to a magazine or club – you don't have to pay anything, and it doesn't add you to a membership list. Subscribing simply tells Navigator you're interested in that particular group. You can then choose to display only the groups of interest, rather than the complete list.

Initially you are subscribed to three newsgroups: `news.announce.newusers`, `news.newusers.questions` and `news.answers`.

1 To subscribe to another group, say `uk.politics`, scroll down the list until you find it, then click in the

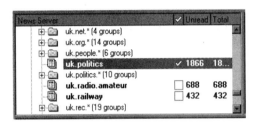

grey box to the right of its name. A yellow tick appears, indicating that Navigator knows you plan to access this group regularly.

REMEMBER

You don't have to subscribe to a newsgroup to read the latest messages. Subscribing is like bookmarking – it simply makes your favourite groups easier to find.

2 You can make the newsgroup list more manageable by showing only the groups you've subscribed to. To

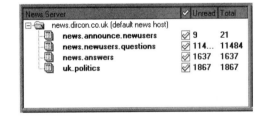

do this, select Show Subscribed Newsgroups from the Options menu.

3 To unsubscribe from a group, click again to remove the tick.

4 To switch back to the complete list, go back to the Options menu and select Show All Newsgroups.

Reading Messages

HANDY TIP

Some groups are very busy and receive hundreds of new messages each day. You can tell Navigator how many headers to download at once by going to the Servers section of Mail and News Preferences and entering a number in the Get: box.

Reading newsgroup messages is just like reading mail (see Chapter Twelve).

1 When you select a newsgroup, Navigator downloads the headers (titles) of all the new messages.

2 Click on a header to display the body of the message in the bottom window.

Threading

Navigator automatically 'threads' newsgroup messages. This means that any message posted in response to another message is displayed immediately below the original. Threading makes it easier to follow the various discussions taking place in a newsgroup.

HANDY TIP

It can take a day or two for a newsgroup message to be copied to every news server. As a result, you'll sometimes see replies to a message before the original reaches your server.

Original message

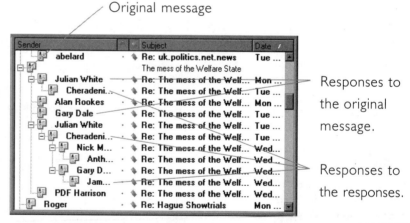

Responses to the original message.

Responses to the responses.

Message Expiry

News messages don't stay on the server indefinitely; your service provider keeps clearing them out to make way for new ones.

The rate at which messages disappear, or 'expire', depends on your service provider. If a group is very busy, any particular message may only be accessible for a day or two; in quieter groups messages expire after one to four weeks.

Posting Messages

You should read pages 148-150 before you start posting messages to newsgroups.

Posting messages is again very similar to sending mail, except you address the message to the newsgroup.

1 To create a new message, select a newsgroup, then click the To: News button or select New News Message from the File menu. The address is added to the Message Composition window automatically.

2 To reply to an existing message, click Re: News or select Post Reply from the Message menu.

3 Again, Navigator brings up a pre-addressed Message Composition window. The original message will usually be quoted (see page 133). Trim it back to a few lines, then add your response at the bottom.

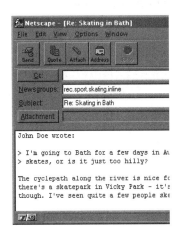

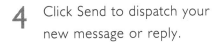

4 Click Send to dispatch your new message or reply.

Private Replies

You can also reply to a message privately, in which case your message goes straight to the author.

HANDY TIP

If your message won't be of interest to anyone else in the newsgroup, send it as a private reply rather than posting it publicly.

1 To reply privately, click the Re: Mail button or select Mail Reply from the Message menu. The original author's e-mail address appears in the Mail To: line of the new message.

2 To reply to both the person and the newsgroup, simultaneously, click the Re: Both button or select Post and Mail Reply from the Message menu.

Netiquette

Usenet has a reputation for being hostile to beginners or 'newbies'. While it's true that some groups are hard to break into, most welcome anyone who displays a little common sense and courtesy. In particular, try to adhere to the following guidelines, known collectively as 'netiquette'.

HANDY TIP

A 'flame' is an abusive message. Some groups tolerate and even encourage flaming; others expect members to be civil. If you post a flame, be prepared to get flamed back!

1 Always read the FAQ (see opposite) before you start posting messages, to avoid (a) posting messages that are inappropriate or (b) asking questions that have already been answered hundreds of times.

2 Don't post the same message to several groups at once. This is known as 'cross-posting', and it irritates the people who end up downloading your message several times.

3 Don't ever post the same message to lots and lots of newsgroups. This is 'spamming', and it irritates everyone. Sadly, you'll encounter lots of spam on Usenet, mostly in the form of ads for moneymaking schemes. Ignore them – responding just makes things worse.

4 If you're replying to a message, don't quote more of the original than is necessary – most people won't want to read it all again. It's helpful to quote the sentence or two you're actually responding to, though.

5 Don't type your message entirely in upper case. This is known as SHOUTING, AND IT MAKES YOUR MESSAGE DIFFICULT TO READ.

FAQs

A FAQ is a compilation of Frequently Asked Questions – and their answers. FAQs exist for two reasons: to set out the group's scope and rules, and to answer all the questions a newcomer might ask.

REMEMBER

'Lurkers' read the messages in a newsgroup, but don't post anything. This is how most people start off – it's a good way to get a feel for what is and isn't acceptable in a particular group.

Most FAQs are posted regularly, generally weekly or monthly. If you 'lurk' in a newsgroup for a while, reading all the messages but not posting anything, the FAQ should eventually appear. You can also find FAQs for many newsgroups at:

```
http://www.cis.ohio-state.edu/hypertext/
faq/usenet/
```

If all else fails, post a polite message asking someone to point you in the right direction. Note that some groups don't have FAQs; others have more than one, and some FAQs serve several groups. If you can't find an appropriate FAQ, lurk for a week or two to get a feel for the group.

Many FAQs represent the collective knowledge of all the members of the newsgroup, and they can be fascinating reading in their own right. The `rec.sport.skating.inline` FAQ, for example, covers everything from buying your first skates to skating backwards down flights of stairs. If you're a coffee drinker, check out the Coffee and Caffeine FAQ, which describes both the substance and the drink in loving detail.

Smileys and Acronyms

Smileys and acronyms speed things up and enable you to clarify your comments.

Smileys

It's difficult to convey emotion in a brief text message. This can lead to misunderstandings, particularly if you're prone to bluntness or sarcasm. As a result many people use 'smileys' – little faces made from keyboard characters – to convey their state of mind.

HANDY TIP

Smileys are also referred to as 'emoticons'. Don't use too many – some people think they're a bit silly.

There are many, many smileys, but the two you're most likely to encounter are:

: -)	happy, or 'only joking'
: - (	sad or disappointed

(Turn the book through 90 degrees to see the faces.)

Acronyms

Common phrases are often abbreviated to just their initials, producing TLAs (Three-Letter Acronyms) and ETLAs (Extended TLAs). You'll also come across a few phonetic abbreviations.

Common acronyms and abbreviations include:

AFAIK	As far as I know
B4	Before
BTW	By the way
F2F	Face to face
FYI	For your information
<g>	Grin
IMHO	In my humble opinion
IMNSHO	In my not so humble opinion
ISTM	It seems to me
ISTR	I seem to recall
IRL	In real life (meaning, off the Internet)
L8R	Later
ROFL	Rolling on floor laughing
RSN	Real soon now
RTFM	Read the (guess) manual

Typical Newsgroups

A few of the alt **groups contain material that is unpleasant, indecent and/or illegal. It's easy enough to avoid them, and you certainly shouldn't assume that all** alt **groups are like this. However, it isn't a good idea to let your children roam about the Internet unsupervised.**

alt.alien.visitors

If you're interested in abductions, conspiracies and all things UFO-related, alt.alien.visitors is the place to start. It appears to be peopled by roughly equal numbers of sceptics and believers, and the lengthy arguments are often quite intriguing. The little green (grey?) men don't seem to be contributing much, though.

alt.comedy.british

The alt.comedy.british newsgroup covers all forms of British comedy, including radio, written and live, but television dominates. Both classic and current series are discussed, generally with warmth and affection. You do sometimes have to explain the jokes to the Americans, but it's a deservedly popular group.

comp.os.ms-windows hierarchy

There are 51 ms-windows groups, covering everything from setting it up to software, utilities and networking. Alternatively, try the 26 comp.sys.ibm.pc groups, which deal with demos, games, hardware and miscellaneous other topics.

rec.arts.startrek.current

There is a theory that the Internet was created to enable *Star Trek* fans to communicate with each other; rec.arts.startrek.current is one of the many places they hang out. The rec.arts.sf.tv hierarchy contains groups for *Babylon 5* and *Quantum Leap*; most other television programmes are still in the alt hierarchy.

rec.ponds

Like most of the specialist rec groups, rec.ponds is either a gold mine or a waste of space, depending on whether you're interested in the subject matter. Whatever your question, someone will have the answer – and be willing to share it with you. It's a friendly group and makes pleasant reading even if you just wish you had a pond. The rec.gardens group covers the rest of your back yard.

rec.sport.soccer

Usenet, like much of the Internet, is dominated by Americans, so the football groups cover American football. If you want football as played in Europe and South America, log on to `rec.sport.soccer` instead. Be prepared for a fairly international view of the game, though.

sci.space.shuttle

The `shuttle` newsgroup covers both the shuttle and the forthcoming international space station. It's peopled mostly by enthusiasts, rather than specialists, so it's more approachable than you might expect. It doesn't have the good looks or real-time features of NASA's Web site (see page 56), but you do get to discuss your ideas rather than just sitting and watching.

soc.couples

The `soc.couples` group covers heterosexual relationships (try `soc.motss` if you're interested in 'members of the same sex'). It's mostly concerned with the niceties of dating and the allocation of chores, and it often makes you realise how wide the Atlantic is – same issues, very different ways of dealing with them.

uk.misc

Reading `uk.misc` is much like listening in on the conversations in your local pub. Current issues dominate, but you can find or start a thread for anything UK-related. You're cutting yourself off from the globalism of the Internet, of course, but sometimes it's nice to join a discussion that isn't dominated by Americans.

uk.politics

If you enjoy discussing the successes and failures of the British Government, try `uk.politics`. Its members are no more likely to reach a consensus than a random selection of MPs, and they can be every bit as belligerent, so be prepared for some lengthy arguments. There are also several subgroups which cover major issues such as the constitution, crime, drugs and the environment.

Index

.net (site) 45
3D worlds 115

A

Acrobat Reader 73, 76, 114
    Plug-in 114
Acronyms 150
Address Book 138
Adobe (site) 57, 76, 114
Adobe PDF files 73, 76, 114
alt newsgroups 143
alt.alien.visitors (newsgroup) 151
alt.comedy.british (newsgroup) 151
Alta Vista (site) 39
Antivirus software 80
Applets 99
Archive files 79
Archives 118
Areas of the screen 22
Articles 142
Attachments 136–137
Audio files 74, 112

B

Back button 27, 96
Backups 80
BBC, The (site) 26, 48
Binaries 143
Bookmark(s) 61–70
    Aliases 67
    Creating 62
    File 68
    Folders 64
    For FTP and gopher sites 126
    Importing 69
    Menu 62–65

Organising 63
Renaming 63
Separators 64
Sorting 67
What's New? 66
Window 63
Broken image icon 33

C

Caches 105–106
Channel 4 (site) 48
Chat sites 94
Check boxes 92
Classic CD (site) 49
Client pull 97
CNN Interactive (site) 42
Colours 104
comp newsgroups 143
comp.os.ms-windows (newsgroup) 151
comp.sys.ibm.pc (newsgroup) 151
Company connections 10, 106
Compressed files 79
Computer Manuals (site) 59
Connecting to the Internet 10–11, 13, 17
Connection software 11, 13
Connections 106
Conservative Party, The (site) 44
Cool Site of the Day (site) 40
Copying text 29
Copyright 30
Credit card details 107
CricInfo (site) 50
Customising Navigator 22
Cyber cafés 10

D

Deleting bookmarks   63
Demon FTP (site)   122
Dial-up connections   11
Direct Connection (site)   60
Directories   38, 86
Directory buttons   22, 86
Directory menu   86
Disconnecting from the Internet   13, 17, 28
Displaying a picture behind the text   104
Document Info   90, 107
Document Source   89
Domain name server   25
Download   14
Downloading
   From FTP sites   120
   Navigator   14
   Newsgroups list   144
   Pages   24
   Programs   78

E

E-mail. *See* Mail
E-zines   45
EarthTime   116
Electronic Gourmet Guide (site)   52
Electronic Telegraph (site)   41
Emap (site)   59
Emoticons   150
Entering URLs   24
Errors   25
Evaluation versions   14–16
Executable files   78

F

FAQs   149
Fastball (site)   51

File extensions

File extensions   73
File Not Found error   25
File Transfer Protocol. *See* FTP
File types   73
Finding text   82
Fixed width font   103
Flames   148
Fonts   103
Forms   92, 108
Forward button   27
Frames   95–96
Freeware   118
FTP   118–124
   Addresses   122
   Connecting to sites   119
   Downloading files   120
   Software   118
   Uploading files   121
Future Publishing (site)   59

G

General Preferences   102–104
   Appearance   27–28, 102
   Colors   104
   Fonts   103
   Helpers   73
   Images   36
Ghostscript   77
Go menu   27
Gopher   125–126
   Addresses   126
   Connecting to sites   126
Grandstand (site)   51
Grooves (site)   32, 49

H

Handbook   87–88
Hayes (site)   57
Help button   102
Help menu   87

Helper applications 71–80, 110
Hewlett Packard (site) 57
History window 84
Home page 27, 68
HotWired (site) 45
HTML 68, 89

I

Image map 35
Images 31–36
Inbox 132–133
Index files 121
inetuk (site) 60
Installing Navigator 16
Installing plug-ins 111
Interactive Web pages 91–100
Internet 8–12
Internet (site) 45
Internet Movie Database (site) 47
Internet service provider. *See* Service
    provider
Internet shortcuts 70
Internet White Pages 86

J

Japan Travel Updates (site) 54
Java 94, 98–99
JavaScript 100
Jazz Online (site) 49

L

Labour Party, The (site) 44
Liberal Democrats, The (site) 44
Licence 20, 87
Licensed version 15, 20
Link icon 22, 66, 70
Links 26, 34, 102, 136–137
Live3D 115
Loading images 33, 96

Location bar 22, 24
Logging off 13
Logging on 13
Lycos (site) 39

M

Macromedia (site) 113
Mail 18, 127–140
    Addresses 128
    Attachments 136–137
    Creating folders 132
    Deleting 134
    Filing 134
    Forwarding 134
    Password 131
    Quoting original message 133–134
    Reading 133
    Receiving 133–136
    Replying to 133
    Sending 129–130, 136–137
Mail and News Preferences
    Composition 133
    Identity 19, 140
    Organisation 131
    Servers 18, 146
Mail Document 137
Mail icon 22, 135
Mail window 131
Mailing lists 139
Mailto: link 129
Main window 22
Man's Life, A (site) 46
MCA/Universal Pictures (site) 47
Media Player 74
Message Composition window 129
Met Office (site) 43
MGM/UA (site) 35, 47
Microsoft (site) 57
Miramax (site) 47
Mirroring 122

Mirsky's Worst of the Web (site)   40
Modems   11
Mozilla   98
Mpeg players   75
Multimedia presentations   113
Multiple main windows   85

N

NASA (site)   56, 75, 85
Natural History Museum (site)   55
Navigator   9
   Customising   22
   Downloading   14
   Installing   16
   Purchasing   15–16
   Running   17
   Upgrading   14
NBA (site)   29, 51
Netiquette   148
Netscape (site)   58, 110, 115
Netscape Communications   9
Netscape Galleria   86
Netscape logo   24, 86, 98
Network Preferences   105–106
   Cache   105
   Connections   106
   Languages   100
   Proxies   106
New Bookmarks folder   65
New Mail Message   130
New Web Browser   85
News. *See* Newsgroup(s)
news newsgroups   143
News window   144
news.announce.newusers
   (newsgroup)   143
Newsgroup(s)   18, 141–152
   Cross posting   148
   FAQs   149
   Flaming   148

List   144
Lurking   149
Main hierarchies   142–143
Message expiry   146
Names   142
Posting to   147
Private replies   147
Quoting original message   147–148
Reading messages   146
Shouting   148
Smileys and acronyms   150
Spam   148
Subscribing to   145
NHL Open Net (site)   51
Nicknames   138
No DNS Entry error   25
No Response error   25

O

Off-line mail   135
On-line services   12
Outbox   132, 135

P

PA NewsCentre (site)   41
Page   22
Paramount (site)   47
Password   93
Pay services   93
PDF. *See* Adobe PDF files
People (site)   95
Phone line   11–12
PKZIP   79
Planet Science (site)   56
Plug-ins   87, 109–116
   Installing   111
Point (site)   40
Points of Presence   12
Politics USA (site)   44
Portico (site)   55

Posts   142
PostScript files   77
Printing pages   28
Project Gutenberg (site)   123
Proportional font   103
Proxies   106
pub folder   119
Public domain software   118
Purchasing Navigator   15–16

Q

Quarterdeck (site)   58
QuickTime for Windows   75

R

Radio buttons   92
RealAudio   112
   (site)   112
rec newsgroups   143
rec.arts.startrek.current
      (newsgroup)   151
Rec.Food.Recipes Archive (site)   52
rec.ponds (newsgroup)   151
rec.sport.soccer (newsgroup)   152
Refresh   83
Registering for a site   93
Registration details   87
Release notes   87
Reloading Web pages   83, 96, 105
RTF files   76
Running Navigator   17

S

Saving files   72, 120
Saving images   33
Saving Location message   120
Saving pages   28
sci newsgroups   143
sci.space.shuttle (newsgroup)   152

Science Museum (site)   55, 89
Search engines   39, 86
Security   100, 107–108
Security logo   22, 107
Self-extracting archive files   79
Sent folder   132
Server   23
Server push   98
Service providers   11–12, 60
Shareware   118
Shocked sites   113
Shockwave   113
Shortcuts. *See* Internet shortcuts
Signature file   140
Site   23
Site registration   93
Sky Internet (site)   48
Smileys   150
Smithsonian (site)   124
soc newsgroups   143
soc.couples (newsgroup)   152
soc.motss (newsgroup)   152
Soccernet (site)   50
Starfish Software (site)   116
Status line   22, 24, 26, 35, 121
Stop button   24
Subscriber to modem ratio   12
SUNET (site)   121–122, 124
SunSITE (site)   119, 122
Support. *See* Technical support
Symantec (site)   57
System requirements   11

T

TCP/IP   13
Technical support
   From Netscape   20, 88
   From service provider   12
Text-only alternatives   33
Threading   146

Thumbnails   34
TimesFax (site)   42, 76
Toolbar   22, 102
Transfer Interrupted message   83
Trash folder   132, 134
Turning off the images   32

U

uk newsgroups   143
uk.misc (newsgroup)   152
uk.politics (newsgroup)   152
Uniform Resource Locators.   *See* URLs
Unipalm PIPEX   15, 20
Unknown File Type message   72
Upgrades   14, 16, 58
Upload   14
Uploading files   121
URLs   23–25
   Abbreviated   23
   Types   23
US Robotics (site)   57
USA Today (site)   42
Useless World Wide Web Pages
      (site)   40
Usenet.   *See* Newsgroup(s)
User name   93

V

Video clips   75
Video for Windows, Microsoft   75
Viewing images   33
Virtual Garden (site)   53, 92
Viruses   80, 100
VRML   115

W

Walt Disney (site)   47, 75
Web   9
Web addresses.   *See* URLs

Web browser   9
Web chat   94
Webcasting   112
Welcome messages   119
What's Cool?   86
What's New?   86
Wine & Dine (site)   52
Winsocks   13, 17
Women's Wire (site)   46
World Wide Web.   *See* Web

Y

Yahoo! (site)   38
YELL (site)   38, 47

Z

Ziff Davis (site)   59
zip files   79